A powerful example of what obedience t
The unreached peoples of the world are
price being paid. This testimony of God's presence in the trial and
the lessons learned will encourage and challenge every reader.

Peter Maiden
International Director Emeritus,
Operation Mobilisation, Oswestry

How we need this book! *Counting the Cost* is the testimony of
medical missionaries David and Shirley Donovan following their
kidnapping in the Niger Delta. During this harrowing ordeal, they
trusted in the bedrock Christian truths of God's sovereign Lordship
over all things, and their heavenly Father's loving care for them in
Jesus Christ. Forgiving enemies, doing good to those who hate, the
sustaining power of the Word of God, and faithfulness unto death
were not simply abstract truths discussed in a classroom. Instead,
they were Christian virtues on full display as they exercised their
faith from day to day. I finished the book praising God for their
courage, and even more, for His all-sufficient grace in our Lord
Jesus Christ.

Charles Wingard
Associate Professor of Practical Theology and
Dean of Students, Reformed Theological Seminary, Jackson

Jesus told His followers to count the cost: no servant is greater than
his master. Christ suffered, and we must be willing to suffer with
Him and for Him. David and Shirley Donovan were willing to risk
personal comfort and security in obedience to Christ. This book is
their testimony to God's goodness in sustaining them through an
ordeal of pain, terror, and uncertainty. They tell the story humbly,
but with an inspiring confidence in God. Reading this is a useful
wake-up call. Where do we put our confidence? In the comforts that
surround us? Or in the living God and His unshakeable promises?

Sharon James
Christian Institute, Newcastle upon Tyne

This gripping book tells a true story of hostage-taking and murder, told first-hand by those who experienced it. It is also the story of how three hostages found God's perspective in a time of great trial from a Bible which they had with them in captivity. I found the book both humbling and a great challenge to complacency.

Alasdair Paine
Vicar, St Andrew the Great, Cambridge
and Trustee of Keswick Ministries

DAVID & SHIRLEY DONOVAN

# COUNTING THE COST

## KIDNAPPED IN THE
## NIGER DELTA

CHRISTIAN
FOCUS

Copyright © David & Shirley Donovan 2019

paperback ISBN 978-1-5271-0306-1
epub ISBN 978-1-5271-0369-6
mobi ISBN 978-1-5271-0370-2

First published in 2019
reprinted in 2019
by
Christian Focus Publications Ltd,
Geanies House, Fearn, Ross-shire,
IV20 1TW, Scotland
www.christianfocus.com

A CIP catalogue record for this book is available
from the British Library.

Cover design by Kent Jensen

Printed and bound by
Bell and Bain, Glasgow

# Contents

Dedicated to the memory of Ian Squire,
Christian brother and very dear friend.

With heartfelt thanks to Julian, Aidan and Patrick.

# PREFACE

If you search for books on heroic travel, solo expedition and accounts of survival and ordeal, you can't help but wonder at man's ability to survive extreme circumstances and the dogged tenacity of the human spirit to overcome adversity.

There are many books that recount truly harrowing tales of kidnap, torture, imprisonment and despair, and the best of these autobiographical or biographical accounts powerfully testify to man's indomitable spirit of survival.

The account told here is not one of these. Neither is it an attempt to somehow spiritualize an ordeal, to add a veneer of Christianity to otherwise bewildering circumstances. Nor is it an attempt to add value to a life lost, that to many may be nothing more than a rogue murder.

The writer of so much of the New Testament, Paul, was a man imprisoned in a shared cell under the might of Roman jurisdiction. It was an empire that spanned three continents, yet within a few hundred years it was a memory, whilst the writings of that frail prisoner were to resonate through the next millennia, establishing the New Testament church that was to lay the foundations of the Judaeo-Christian heritage of the free world. The world looks for evidence of a God. Many wonder at creation, but in a post-Christian, secular world, the Bible and the claims of Christ are considered an anathema.

Sometimes the road to faith comes through the expressed testimony of others. Paul and the psalmist state that 'we believe, therefore we speak'. This book is a testimony, of a conviction of God that led one man to give of his life, and the remaining to tell of the events. The testimony is to present the account, unblemished. It must point to the reason for faith, and that is the person of Jesus Christ, the Word of God made flesh.

There is no commercial gain to be taken by the authors of this book. All royalties go to sustain the work of New Foundations Medical Mission that continues in the remote creeks of the Niger Delta, to witness that, though empires and theories will come and go, the Word of God will last forever. It is for the reader to decide if there is reason to examine further the person of Jesus Christ.

The narrative chapters are David's voice, the chapters which expand the spiritual 'lessons' are Shirley's voice. 'We' is employed when an experience or perception is shared. Biblical quotations are from the English Standard Version (ESV).

# 1
# INTRODUCTION

It had been eight months since we had last been with our team.

We had never been away for this long, though there were almost daily telephone calls. For the preceding three years we had gently hinted and prepared them for this day, when either illness, political change, or the unexpected may preclude our return and they would have to manage on their own.

In some way it was like visiting our sons in their first flat, to see how they were managing with independence and the associated responsibilities it brings.

After seven years providing face to face medical care, we had gradually stepped back infilling with our workers as we concentrated on their training and mentoring to work independently. Now fourteen years on we visited the work for encouragement, discipling, and to review the Mission programmes every three to four months. On both sides this extended gap had been a testing time. Working cross-culturally, despite the common bonds of the Christian faith, had nevertheless taught us never to take things for granted and to always realize your brother or sister in Christ may still be filtering what they see, and what they hear, through a prism of want, of tradition, aspiration, colour, tribe, or tongue that's so often taken us by surprise.

Even after all these years there is always the last-minute phone call for emergency items such as German spark plugs for the outboard engine, fuel hoses for a chainsaw, anti-epileptic medication that cannot be found locally. Frantic hours on eBay or medical supply sites sometimes proved productive, but the perception remained that here in the U.K. everything was immediately to hand. I guess from the perspective of most in Nigeria this was in fact reasonable. As the days drew to each departure the familiar grey holdalls began to be filled to their twenty-three-kilogram limit and stacked in our hallway. Every bag was weighed to the gram. With over forty-five trips or more, we had this down to a fine art. Every allowance was utilized. The bags were full to bursting for the outward flight. We returned with only the lightest of hand luggage to speed through check-in and customs, notoriously unpredictable and tortuous at Port Harcourt Airport.

So often in Christian mission, the first casualty is prayer and spiritual preparation. It's so easy to get lost in the fog of equipment needs, travel arrangements, and logistics. We've learned this the hard way, with countless disappointments and difficulties along the way which have driven us back to questioning our whole purpose in going. We have learnt that prayer is critical, and to be sure that the call to go is genuine, of God, and for His glory, and not for our own ego, and pursuit of adventure.

We were looking forward to spending time with Ian, our mission partner, who ran in tandem his own evangelical Christian mission, taking Eye Care as a vehicle for the gospel to remote regions of Africa. He had been with us many times, and this time Alanna, a young optometrist, was joining him – her first time on short-term mission. Many times it was just Shirley and I, and inevitably, with no escape from each other or a mediator to bring humour into difficult situations, trips could be emotionally tiring and intense.

Despite the promise of a fuller trip with friends old and new, Shirley had almost shut herself down for the preceding weeks before the trip, spending little time with friends. Not knowing herself the reason, she had been spending much more time Bible-reading, and in prayer and quiet reflection.

The Niger Delta will, I suspect, never be a holiday destination, and I cannot think of any time that we have relished the prospect of going, knowing the volatility of the area, the physical isolation and lack of amenities. Cerebral malaria had put a friend in intensive care and almost killed Shirley. Foreign Office guidance and travel insurance always necessitate a kidnapping premium of a thousand pounds a week; small wonder then that we had never seen a white face in the creeks where God had called us to.

The Bible tells us to rejoice in tribulation. Despite the difficulties, there has always been a great joy being with our team and seeing how God works so tangibly and unexpectedly in such a difficult environment, when nothing should bear fruit yet, according to His divine purpose, does.

Nevertheless, Shirley had a sense of unease preceding this trip which is easy to ascribe in hindsight but was inexplicable at the time. For myself I had felt the timing was difficult as my mother was in the final stages of terminal cancer and there was the very real possibility of her dying before our return. Deciding to go was difficult. At ninety-five the end could come at any time, but she was in good spirits, alert and stable. We had talked and agreed that a short trip, so long in the planning, would be fine – a calculated risk worth taking. She was so supportive of the work.

We did not know, but Ian, like Shirley, was also reluctant to go, and had confided in a mutual friend that he felt that this would be his last trip to Nigeria. He had said to me previously that he felt he had done everything he could in terms of teaching the staff, and there was a restlessness to free himself of constraints in his own life, to streamline his own mission to something far more spontaneous and grassroots. He had a restlessness to draw closer to God and felt the governance and administrative burdens of running a registered charity were encumbrances he wished to shed.

We met as usual at the check-in desk at Air France in terminal four at Heathrow at 5 a.m. It was cold, and still dark outside. Alanna had joined Ian the previous evening. She did look very young, we thought. Shirley confided that she looked like a gap-year student out for an adventure, a comment she would later apologize for.

Leo, another friend, was joining us for the trip; he was a serious Christian brother we had known just a short time but who was keen to visit the Mission.

After the countless bags were checked in and the short hop to Charles de Gaulle, the longer flight to Port Harcourt via Abuja gave some time for prayer and reading and preparation.

Shirley was reading the Bible and felt God draw her to the book of Revelation 3:1-2, where God remonstrates against the church of Sardis. 'I know your works. You have the reputation of being alive, but you are dead. Wake up, and strengthen what remains and is about to die, for I have not found your works complete in the sight of my God'. After eight months since our last visit, Shirley felt sure that this confirmed that there was lack of governance in the work, and a number of shortcomings which would need to be addressed.

The Niger Delta is a land of paradox. A land worthy of being demarcated as a UNESCO World Heritage site for its mangroves and forests, it also boasts some of the most spectacularly polluted areas of the world. Since oil was discovered in the middle of the last century, Western interest has fought over the massive oil reserves, at its peak rocketing Nigeria to the seventh biggest oil producer in the world.[1]

---

1. OPEC Report 2014.

The politics of the Delta are tortuous. Put simply, much of the land was bought at agricultural prices, the communities unaware of what stratospheric wealth lay beneath their feet. Their birthright sold, oil companies poured in sinking oil wells throughout the region, sometimes the only hint of such activity being a thinly disguised painted green wellhead from which large pipes run out to eventually reach pumping stations at the coast. It's a curious site to see a corroding wellhead producing millions of dollars weekly, sitting cheek by jowl with a timeless scene of a dugout canoe moored to a thatch hut. Built on stilts, a naked child squats on the edge of the rickety structure, and defecates. In the brackish water and ebbing tide, the nutrient-rich mud is slowly exposed, and mud skippers come out from their burrows to feed.

The main oil fields are situated in the most remote regions of the Delta, toward the Atlantic. Up to 100 miles offshore, large, foreign-owned oil rigs light superflares, burning off the gas and emitting billions of cubic metres of carbon dioxide. As a night flight takes off from Port Harcourt Airport and slowly banks northwards, the view from the windows shows a myriad of fires dotting the jungle and out to sea in a number too many to count. The oil flaring is almost beyond comprehension. Eduardo, a helicopter pilot from Chile, recounted how he could feel the heat from a superflare through the plexiglass of his helicopter up to a mile away. As clouds passed over these flares they literally evaporated. While the emissions of sulphur and carbon dioxide went unchecked, below his helicopter rainbow ribbons of oil sneaked through the creeks from sabotaged oil pipelines. Eduardo took pictures of these oil slicks on his phone, and scrolling through them, it was easy to see how all the snaking tendrils of surface oil polluted and decimated fish stocks and drinking water.

Already the carrier of so much disease, the brackish waters of those communities nearest the Atlantic were as good as dead. As you wander around the communities, corrugated tin roofing is rusted and heavily corroded. With all the gas emissions and flaring, the rain in this region is acidic and injurious to both health and environment.

Eduardo joked that he recently saw a satellite television show extolling the British love of recycling and organic gardening. As he recounted the interview with a green-fingered organic gardener promoting organic composting by worms to save the environment, he drilled his forefinger to his temple. 'Have these people any idea?' he said. 'Look around you, look at what is going on; it's a madhouse.' I thought of Gardeners' Question Time in the light of what he had shown me, and true, it seemed like a parallel universe.

In many ways the Delta is the frontier of corporate exploitation and organized crime, impossible to police and porous to any policies of good governance. Corruption is endemic at every level from community to government, and harder to eradicate than Japanese knotweed. The basic problem of course is greed – corporate, community, and personal.

Something that is pervasive in the corrosive humidity of the Niger Delta is the lack of attention to maintenance and servicing of equipment. This seems true in much of West African society where there is just not the infrastructure, planning and re-sourcing to maintain initiatives that begin well but are not underpinned by adequate training, funding and accountability.

Nowhere perhaps evidences this better than the arrivals hall at Port Harcourt Airport. Year upon year it garners the dubious award by voting travellers as the worst international airport in the world.[2] The much-trumpeted new arrivals hall has lain for years as a simple concrete skeleton, black with mould, with trees now growing from fractured joints in the structure. The current 'arrivals hall' is a vast dirty grey tent,

---

2. No. 1 in a global survey of 26,000 travellers: 'sleepinginairports.net' 2015, and ranked 3rd in 2017, across several key indices – security, customs, navigation, etc.

once white, with at present a second generation of roller banners swaying precariously, promising a world-class facility and the strap line of 'Please bear with us for the inconvenience'.

The whole experience of arriving at Port Harcourt is so miserable that one chooses a seat on the left-hand side of the aeroplane, so it gives you the chance of disembarking a little earlier to the front door on the same side. After a sweat-drenched scurrying across the tarmac you are corralled into an open-sided passage with an awning, where, contrary to every political sensibility in western liberalism, 'whites' are lined on the right and paused until all African nationalities have passed through. Arrival cards with minuscule text are completed under the glow of mobile phones, as the flight arrives after sunset and there is no lighting in the dismal passageway. After a moment or two a haze of mosquitoes gathers in the glow of the mobile phone. After shuffling into the tent, an infrared camera takes your temperature, a throwback to the Ebola crisis some years back, and with a pervading sense of disapproval and suspicion, passports are checked and rechecked. Another official checks the yellow-fever certificate as our row shuffles towards the immigration desk. To one side an Italian oil worker has been hauled outside due to an expired yellow-fever certificate. After some remonstrating, calm is re-established and it is clear to all in the queue that money has changed hands. The immigration officers know they carry absolute power. Unlike almost any other country there is really no plan B available to those travelling out with multinational company cover. As for us, it has been amazing that we have never given way to blackmail and extortion over the years, God making a way in every situation.

Once clear and the bags collected from an opening in the side of the tent, there comes the supreme task of running the gauntlet of the customs officers. For a small donation checks can be avoided, and there is a constant request for a little gift or similar, to ease one's passage through this stressful process. More so than the U.K. there is a real deference to the office held in Nigeria. Whilst this reinforces organizational hierarchy, it is also because of this deference that abuse of office is so widespread, as there seems no machinery to bring miscreants to book.

The influence of Christianity remains strong in Nigeria, and to present official papers confirming that the Mission is Christian and registered with the government both in the U.K. and Nigeria, always pours oil on an otherwise fraught situation. It's never lost on those who travel with us to the Delta region, this respect for God's Word, and how it seems to trump any personal agenda. It is ironic however, that this respect for the professing Christian and seeming identity with them does nothing to deter officials from petty bribery and intimidation. It's probably fair to say that in the Niger Delta a profession of faith in Christ and having the right piece of paper when challenged will normally get you out of most sticky situations. Perhaps that's why the currency of 'christianisms' and well-chosen verses have been so misused and abused. It's not unusual to hear on the public bus young people, who by music and conversation have both feet in the world, nevertheless competing with each other to see who can recite the most verses of the Bible.

Finally clearing customs, the next hurdle is the metal fence where throngs of shadowy faces wave arms offering phone cards, taxis or more shady deals. Victory Okuboarere, our Mission Superintendent, God-fearing and ever reliable, pushes through the crowd to meet us.

'Mummy Shirley, Doctor Sir, you are welcome, how is the family over there?'

He smiles broadly, his eyes dancing. Some of the female workers say he has 'lady teeth' because they are so big, so white and so straight.

'So good to see you, Victory, everyone's fine. Is Charles nearby?'

'Yes Sir, I'll call him now, to come. Ah, we praise God you are here safely.' He grinned once more insisting to take a case from me.

As we weaved our way to the minibus, a variety of young men clung to us seeking change, offering assistance, having waited all day and in the heat for the final incoming flight that may bring some foreign change.

It was a joy to see Victory again and despite everyone lashed in sweat, the hugs are genuine. This young man had stayed the course – he had a servant heart. One day when it was lashing with rain at our clinic, I apologized that I needed him to make a telephone call. It was raining heavily, windy and dark outside. He donned a cagoule.

At the door he turned and gently spoke, 'It is not a problem, I'm doing it for God, not for you.'

Port Harcourt is the major oil hub in southern Nigeria, having gained the crown from neighbouring Warri, a city four hours to the west. Militant unrest and armed incursion into the city in the early 2000s meant many companies moved their operations to Port Harcourt. The pendulum is swinging the other way now and Port Harcourt is rife with hostage taking and carjacking. As a westerner you would be a fool to stay in any hotel that did not have armed guards and twenty-four-hour protection.

The traffic in the city is nightmarish, and to stray from the main roads is dangerous. A simple ten-mile drive can take up to three hours and arriving at the hotel behind the sliding steel gates is a huge relief. Doubling as a rather louche gentleman's club at the weekends with an agonizing cover-band poolside, it is safe and the food reliable. It's a depressing sight to see so many late-middle-aged men from western Europe escorting girls young enough to be their daughters. Loneliness and alcohol are a malign mixture, and to risk their own health and those of their families at home for a moment of pleasure is sad and pathetic.

More so, however, is the need of these young girls that they should have to sell themselves in this way. The night porter announces he is also a Pastor and in the same breath declares he is on the lookout for a western wife. He asks for phone numbers and Facebook contacts.

The staff are pleasant, and Shirley has brought two prints of photos she took of the reception staff on the last trip. With pleasantries exchanged and enquiries of each family made, sleep is welcome and immediate, despite the blistering refrain of 'Wind Beneath My Wings' coming from the pool bar.

The drone of the air-conditioning cannot combat the noise of the early morning rush hour, and departure was set for 9 a.m. Leaving Port Harcourt, the detritus of Prosperity teaching is plastered across every huge billboard that lines the major roads. News of a three-day supernova prayer-quake emblazoned against an erupting volcano competes against another church, promising the attendees a guaranteed year of jubilee. Another church admonishes its congregation with the words 'Jesus never misses a service here', whilst another proclaims the credentials of the lead Pastor as 'the destroyer of Demons and the Bishop to the universe'. More modest churches display vast hoardings depicting the lead Pastor and his wife in thoughtful pose with chin resting between the thumb and forefinger, somehow de rigueur with all aspiring singers, Pastors, politicians and technocrats. It seems shorthand for a seriousness and intentionality of purpose. It must be bamboozling for a serious Christian seeking sound teaching to navigate the mountebanks and charlatans selling their corporate wares. Yet in each of these churches it must be true that there are Christians of all shades who are true followers of Christ, who are fainting for real spiritual food and fellowship.

As the billboards begin to space out and the city slides away, the next hurdles are the roadblocks coming sometimes every two or three miles, manned by the army, the joint task force, the police and the traffic police. Elsewhere 'Area boys' and local gangs stand ready to throw out planks peppered with nails. They mean business, but a little change usually suffices to gain safe passage.

Though these desperate men and officials stop nearly every car and truck for the sole intention of extracting money, they will always respond favourably to the offer of prayer instead of payment. Many young soldiers have families and are paid very little. Levying this small informal tax is seen by many as a justifiable perk of the job. When stopped at gunpoint, Shirley declined to pay but took the young man's hands and prayed for him and his family. He was visibly moved, his grip softening as she prayed that he would find the reality of Christ in his life such greater value than the derisory sums he was gathering from the passing traffic.

Another time a gang of middle-aged men armed with spiked planks stopped the car, but after an exchange and expressing the very real grievance of poverty and lack, they themselves requested prayer rather than money. This clearly had a profound effect as the next few times the driver was stopped by them, they let him pass, enquiring of their good friends who had taken the time to pray with them.

Such is the confusion of Port Harcourt and its environs. Such is the power of God to touch even the hardest hearts amidst the noise and chaos.

As the major roads give way to minor and the thick jungle or 'de boosh' (as spoken in pidgin) slowly takes dominance in the landscape, tarmac gives way to sand and the electric light bulb to the kerosene lamp. The motor car reaches the end of the track where the New Foundations team wait to greet us. For the last few kilometres Victory had been texting them of our imminent arrival. The sun is burning, the humidity high, but how delightful to be with the brothers and sisters in Christ, some of whom we have known for fifteen years.

The bags are transferred from the car to the clinic boat, a simple open fibreglass boat with a 40 horsepower engine. Across the river wait the rest of the team, who break out into a self-penned welcome song as we all disembark. Some local fisherwomen run over from their dugout canoes to say hello. Some are recognized, many are not. But at some point, the clinic at Enekorogha had rescued their children from accident or overwhelming infection. The bond of simple gratitude draws them close.

The ragged line of workers, the newly arrived team and skipping children, winds its way across the field outside the semi-derelict secondary school toward the mission station and farm set at the very edge of the bush to the rear.

The excitable greetings and pressure of new faces and new demands make it easy to be drawn into others' agendas and a world in chaos. We close the door on the community, who quietly fade away, and turn our attention to the very real need to seek God in this alien and difficult place. After many years providing a boat service to communities, God showed us clearly that to have any lasting impact in the area, we needed to commit to a community. The ruinous clinic at Enekorogha, situated by the river and visible to all passing boats was given over to the Mission by the State Department of Health, a gift from God that released us from building a structure with all the associated costs and hurdles.

The name 'Enekorogha' translated means 'the place you cannot stay', but God had been faithful over the past ten years, such that the local elders were seeking to add a suffix to the name with the new meaning, 'the place you can always stay'.

Vivian had produced her customary pasties, prepared from the most basic of stone ovens, and a crate of minerals [sic] sat in the centre of the room from where Coke or Fanta was passed around, the tops popped off by workers' teeth.

Familiar choruses and worship songs gave way to a time of praise and prayer; and Shirley had a particular sensitivity to the Holy Spirit who showed her many things during these times. African praise and singing can often descend into formula and theatre. The dancing and clapping can beguile the western Christian unaccustomed to such exuberance, but over the years, sensitivity to the nuance of body language and demeanour in particular, highlighted those workers who were struggling both in their faith and calling.

Medicine had always been the vehicle for the gospel and where the occasional worker had become entangled, in usually sexual sin, a cooling heart towards Christ had always been the first step. I once commented to a local Pastor who was serious about his faith and mentored the workers, that his church seemed thriving with close on two hundred people.

'No,' he said quietly, 'I pastor a church of six people, the other hundred and ninety-four come for entertainment', a perceptive if rather depressing observation. It was equally true in mission that one or two value their job for the salary it brings, and out of the twenty-eight workers maybe eight or nine had chosen this poorly paid and demanding work because they sincerely sought to serve their God by the word of their testimony and in the witness of delivering compassionate healthcare.

Shirley was upset after the opening time of prayer, worship and devotion. She felt in her spirit that many were cold in their faith. One or two prayed with their eyes open gazing around, and prayer for some was perfunctory and rote. Even Ian had wanted to get on with the teaching of the Eye Care, as this camp was short, and he had to conduct their final examination. Perhaps it's a gender issue but I also had to fight back those practical demands on my time, and it is God-ordained that there is a very real strength having a helpmate in these situations. God profoundly used Shirley to ensure the priority was submitting to and seeking the face of God before all else on arrival.

The next day we visited the clinic to review the work. The gospel is preached daily before all activities. The pharmacy, laboratory and morning clinics were running well and a steady flow of patients came and went. In the ward, however, a mother lent over a child connected to a drip. Shirley looked around the ward; workers were present but milling aimlessly around, seemingly blind and indifferent to the mother and child. She called me to come and look at the child. 'Why is there no one attending to this child?'

Shirley went to call the senior workers. The gravity of the situation was obvious.

'What's going on with this child? Get me his notes, who's meant to be in charge? There is no one I can see, looking after this child.'

There was a general flurry and his admission file was thrust into my hand. The 'clerk-in' was competent, the diagnosis seemed reasonable and the initial treatment competent. Observations had been taken half hourly overnight but then suddenly at 6 a.m. the observations had ceased and during this time the child had obviously deteriorated precipitously.

Victory had come in the room to see what the commotion was. I pointed at the child. 'Victory what should be done?'

'Oh, this is serious, he has the danger sign of a coma,' and, squeezing his cold hands and feet, added, 'I think he has septicaemia.'

'Well what drugs is he on?'

'Ceftriaxone, and, erm, quinine for malaria.'

'Victory, come on, do you think it's safe to leave this child here?'

'No Sir,' he shook his head, 'he should be transferred immediately.'

'Thank heavens, absolutely. This should have been done before now. Can you explain the situation to the mother and tell her we will transport the child by boat? Tell her to go and get her husband and come back immediately to the jetty.'

The mother looked panicked, having had no idea how sick her child was, and dashed from the ward. There was no time and sadly, despite reaching the regional hospital, the child succumbed to the overwhelming infection a few hours later.

When the child had left I re-examined the admission sheet. There was an obvious inconsistency in the final, recorded oxygen saturation, blood pressure and pulse. If true, then the child would have been close to death, yet the written care-plan stated otherwise. 'Whose handwriting is this?' I asked tersely.

Charity, a young worker, leant over, 'Mm, Shakespeare's, Sir.'

Shakespeare was called and grilled over his entries in the notes. Realizing he was backed into a corner, he conceded that he had fabricated the last readings as he had been up all night and had gone to bed exhausted, failing to hand over to the next shift. Charity had popped her head in once or twice but had not bothered to check the child or properly read the medical notes. If she had done so, the error would have been clear to see. This was all avoidable, so frustrating, so maddening. What started well like so many other things, simply tailed off through indolence and indifference, the child paying for this with its life and a mother overwhelmed by grief.

The plans for the day were scrapped, the workers being summoned to the bungalow to review this critical incident. I stood in the centre of the circle unapologetically livid. Each worker was given a sheet of paper and told to go away and write a pro forma for admitting a sick child, citing details of history, examination and investigations.

The group was re-gathered later in the afternoon and sheepishly each worker handed in their work. Even on a cursory glance some sheets were creased, messy and sparse in content. I inwardly groaned. Only five sheets resembled anything half acceptable and Shirley held nothing back, coming down hard on the workers' flippancy.

'Do you think it's acceptable to hand in work like this?' she said holding up and shaking one of the papers. She had a tremor in her voice.

'Do you really care so little and have such little respect for the fact that we've travelled three days to get here and that you think it's acceptable to dash off a few lines because you can't be bothered to do it properly? Well, do you?' Her voice was shaking with both disappointment and fury.

'Well, I for one will not accept this, so go away and do this again.' It was incredible that even one of the senior workers had thought herself above the need to submit anything at all.

As we look back, God's hands were so clearly in this messy situation. God was visibly separating the sheep from the goats right before our very eyes.

The next day acceptable papers were handed in by each worker, but their cover had been blown. God had showed us so clearly those few workers who had a heart for service and commitment to the vision of the work. Maybe the best paper of the initial five was from Vivian, who had been toiling in the kitchen and undertook her assignment simultaneously sitting on a tiny stool as she cooked. As she said herself, she was doing it unto the Lord.

The atmosphere at the mission station was still awkward and sour, and most members of the team had withdrawn into small huddles in the bedrooms. Ian and Alanna had begun teaching at the clinic with Leo observing. As so often, the vast meeting room at the mission station was empty, the ghostly imprints of some of the workers still indented into the beanbags, and Bibles, pens and mobile phones scattered around the room.

So much of our time on the Mission is spent at a home-made table gazing at the jungle and at each other, despairing of the relentless one-step-forward-two-steps-back nature of it all. As the mid-afternoon thunderstorm lashes the palm trees and the rain falls like marbles being dropped on the zinc roof, it's hard to hear one another speak. This can be a blessing at times like this. As the rain eases, the light turns a curious orange against the green of the jungle and the temperature falls by a welcome degree or two. It is exhausting both physically and mentally.

Coffee plays a crucial role, a small reminder of home. Once again, like most trips, by the end of the first day we are spiritually and emotionally wrung dry. How apposite are the words to the church in Sardis that God should 'know your works, that you have the reputation of being alive, but are dead.' It seemed to both of us that these words had been confirmed this day.

This was to prove to be only the beginning.

# 2
# TAKEN HOSTAGE

The last night of every camp is euphemistically called Gala night. One young man who joined us commented he had never seen such laughter and disinhibition in the absence of alcohol and mind-altering drugs. A rhythm section can spontaneously arise from a spoon on an empty Coke bottle, and syncopation of hand clapping that is completely impossible to follow despite the years of practice. A communal meal of jollof rice, chicken or donkey hide and, when available, catfish, takes a day to prepare and is demolished in minutes. A crate of Coke and Fanta accompanies the meal, the bottle tops wrenched off by two of the workers using their teeth. Testimony, worship and praise can move from a spontaneous conga to each worker encouraged to give testimony or song. For some, the excitement is just too much. Rose, one of the senior workers, unable to contain herself, falls to the floor and rolls backwards and forwards shrieking 'Hallelujah' in unfettered joy. The mood abruptly changes as Florence, a young mother who had lost five of her children, sang a beautiful self-penned song called 'The Storm Is Over', as she surfaced from yet another season of grief, beautiful, heartfelt and so poignant.

A cheap desktop disco light dances circles of colour around the vast parlour, and everyone arrives in traditional outfits and with a sense of expectancy. For us, however, the best we can normally muster at the end of a camp is a clean T-shirt and for Shirley, a new African wrap.

This camp, however, had been different. Much of the preceding week had been problematic. Both Ian and Leo had suffered fevers and gastroenteritis; and Ian had struggled to get all the training done so his three Eye Care students could sit their final exam on the last day.

With the child's death on the day of arrival, illness and an exhausting schedule, we decided a meal and a film would give a quieter end to the camp. The film recounted the crucifixion from the point of view of the centurion – mentioned in Matthew 27:54 – who declared that the crucified Jesus was indeed the son of God. All the workers were transfixed and lived every moment, interjecting with outrage at every character who denounced Christ. This was not entertainment, they were actually living the experience.

The two workers who had passed their exam sat on beanbags clutching their framed certificates with huge grins as they watched the film. The third, who failed by only a few points, was sanguine, and sat with his classmates, his eyes occasionally wandering from the film to the shiny certificates he had missed out on.

By the end of the film one or two of the workers had fallen asleep, tired and post-prandial. As the credits rolled, those asleep were nudged awake. A heap of extension leads feeding various mobile phones and rechargeable torches were winking red and green indicating that all were fully charged; and as the workers left, they collected what was theirs, the beams of the torches amidst the fireflies helping them navigate the muddy path back to the clinic for either sleep or, for the unlucky, the nightshift.

Vivian and two colleagues swept the floor of fishbones, bottle tops, sand and grit from bare feet, spilt rice and the odd ant. The chairs were placed back in the circle for devotions at 7 a.m., the beanbags puffed up and arranged around the central upright beam of the room, that in truth held up the entire roof. (When it rains the force of the water and the volume did make me think we should have put in another one or two, a concern that was now too late and a niggling worry I kept to myself.)

Victory, the Mission Superintendent, had called Charles, our driver, earlier in the evening. In truth he was the cousin of a hotel receptionist we once enquired of for a taxi. Sensing a deal, she directed us to Charles rather than the hotel taxi. Charles was a thoughtful intelligent man, a devout Christian who maintained his car with rigour, such that it passed muster with even the most forensic traffic policeman seeking to leverage a fine from an impromptu road block. As always, he confirmed he would be on the other side of the creek at 10 a.m. with his car.

I had scurried around collecting cables and the mass of electronics we tend to bring; and in our bedroom our hand luggage bags were only half packed as there would be time in the morning to finish.

'Oh, come on, just leave things and get to bed,' Shirley said. 'It's too late to do all that now.' She had showered and was already under the mosquito net, tucking it in under the mattress.

For years we had borrowed accommodation, sometimes dividing sleeping into women's and men's bedrooms, without electricity and the ability to wash, and sleeping on beds where we all had to turn in unison. Water had to be sourced from the river and was stored in empty oil drums or a rusty tank. After showering with a small plastic cup from the barrel, you sometimes smelt of rust with the little orange hue on the skin.

Once, fed up with this, I went to bathe in the river. The moon was out, there was a gentle current, and the water was virtually body temperature – it seemed perfect.

Waking the next day, there were oil stains on the mattress and several invertebrates wriggling around in various states of demise. Pollution is endemic in this area from sabotaged oil pipelines, and small spots of crude stick like glue to your skin as a psychedelic slick slowly leaches down the river decimating shellfish and livelihoods. The Pastor was amused that I had bathed in the river and commented that he had just 'mashed' a four-foot watersnake at the very same spot five minutes after I had got out. Never again. To now have a mission station with your own bedroom, bathroom, with borehole water and a toilet was a luxury, never to be taken for granted.

I locked the door, peering through the spy hole. The large parlour was quiet with the night workers sprawled over the sofas, ready to refuel the generator that provided the fans and the floodlighting around the building. The mission station was within yards of the jungle and at the very end of the community. Behind the eight-foot wall and steel gates, the metal doors were locked and every window covered by an iron grill, the floodlights illuminating every nook and cranny in the compound. The clouds of insects around each light buzzed and fizzled until dawn.

I showered, turned the 'Ox' – our large floor-standing fan – to cyclone mode and, switching off the lights, zipped up the mosquito net. Like a hospital curtain around the bed it gave the illusion of security and privacy. The petroleum smell of insecticide spray, still heavy, hung in the air, but at least the carcasses of the insects on the floor testified that the place was safe. It's too hot to sleep with clothes or a sheet, and the fan whips the hot and humid air around us.

Before sleep there was a chance to reflect on the day, to read the Bible and most importantly to bring concerns and worries before the Lord. Sometimes lying there with the sound of the generator, the insects and the surrounding jungle, you can feel particularly alone. The barrier of language and culture and distance and vulnerability can whisper despair at what foolishness it is to keep labouring in this place, so often with little results. Some problems can seem insurmountable, and the conscious laying down of these concerns was a reminder that this was foremost a work by and for the glory of God, and that as humans you can, as the African proverb says, 'Only do what you can do'. Our call is simply to be obedient, but the fruits and the harvest will always be of the Lord. To take ownership of the work would be disastrous and destructive. There's a danger that missionaries feel validated by their work and calling. Like a little leaven an honest calling to the mission field can slide into a 'good work', despite the best of intentions. As humans we can get so allured by the process. Our validation must always be in Christ and only as we lay ourselves down in full surrender can Christ be made manifest through our lives. This was something we perhaps partially understood but were later to understand in its totality.

The whole house was silent but for the steady and reassuring rhythm of the Lister generators. Lying on the mattress, the last moisture from the shower cooling us in the breeze of the oscillating fan, we lay in reverie, jotting down mentally things to do before departure in the morning. The day done, the camp concluded successfully, sleep came almost instantly, welcome and deep...

...The pounding on the door was furious and had urgency. Shirley awoke and sat bolt upright. She shook me.

'What's that?' she said.

She had no need, for we both knew instantly.

'Come on, get up, quick, get dressed.'

We frantically unzipped the mosquito net, and Shirley reached for the light switch, flicking it up and down.

'Power's off ... where's the torch?' I was panting, the adrenaline starting to surge.

'Dunno, just find some clothes.'

I knelt in the blackness, sweeping the floor frantically with my hands backwards and forwards in the darkness for some clothes to put on. The fan stood still and silent. Without the drone of the fan and the rhythm of the generator, the crashing on the front door was loud, monstrous and frightening. We scrambled around the floor, our breathing rapid and shallow.

With a sudden explosive crash, there was silence.

A second or two later the pounding began again, rhythmic and intentional.

I had found some running shorts and, fumbling, I pulled them on. My body was soaked in sweat and I was shaking. My hands ran into Shirley's and, like blindmen, we ran our fingers to and fro over the half-packed cases for clothes, now panicking. The pounding again had stopped and then a brutal crash just feet from our door told us somebody was attacking the adjacent bedroom door and would soon be at ours. It was as if a wild monster was rampaging in the house, and in a sense this was true, demonic and ungodly.

Within seconds a crash shuddered our door and after three more it gave, bursting open. Shafts of light flashed in faces as three men lunged into the room, huge black silhouettes, their torches flashing around the room as they shouted

'Quick, move, move, move!'

Their pump-action shotguns and AK-47s flashed into view as the torch beams passed across them. They were pointing them at us. One bent down, having spied my laptop and gathering it up whilst shouting at us to get out. Shirley stood vulnerable, her eyes screwed up against the light in her face, dressed only in a bra and pair of trousers.

She spotted a fleeced top and reached for it before one of them kicked it away shouting, 'No!' The voice was low and guttural.

Their faces were covered. Our vision was half blinded by the torchlight, but as I looked down, I saw their wellington boots and oil workers' waterproof trousers. My arm was grabbed, and I was pushed first from the bedroom. Shirley had less than a second to grab a wrap, which she saw on the floor beside her, and then was shoved from the darkness to the empty, silent parlour.

The front door was open, and jittery torchlight showed there was activity outside. On the step outside, Johnson, one of the lads charged with looking after the generator, sat rocking, praying softly but audibly, his hands clutching his bloody head. His shirt was muddy and torn.

Alanna and Ian stood silent and expressionless at the bottom of the steps, the whiteness of their skin shining against the black silhouetted gunmen who stood beside them, stark in the white LED torch beams. Ian stood in shorts and a T-shirt. Alanna in her nightwear, a white T-shirt and shorts. We were corralled together, flanked on either side by gunmen who, with agitated excitable breathing, pushed us hurriedly to the front gates of the compound which had been forced open.

Behind us the mission station was in darkness, almost invisible against the brooding silence of the jungle.

The caretaker's house was silent and without the light of a torch anywhere. Almost ten people remained in the mission station unarmed and fearful. The female workers had hid because rape was so often the consequence of being discovered. Leo, our other friend, was sleeping in the other section of the mission station, and it was immediately clear they had targeted our three rooms and must have had an informant to know how to cut the generator and to find us so quickly and efficiently.

Barefooted we stumbled across the granite chippings that strewed the path to the gate, unseen hands pushing us forcefully from behind.

The community was deathly quiet. How different it is in the daytime when children run up to touch with curiosity your skin, and feel the smooth hair, to smile and joke. Friends and members of the community whom we have known or have travelled with through sickness and calamity would greet us on the back roads through the jungle.

Now it was pitch black, alien and menacing, with only the cacophony of courting toads on the wet, muddy, secondary-school field and the heavy breathing and grunting of our captors, who pushed and shoved us in the direction of the river. Did people know what was happening but were too afraid to come to our rescue? Or were they asleep, unaware that 'their people' were being kidnapped right beneath their noses? It mattered not, no help was forthcoming. Before us the engorged River Niger flowed south to the Atlantic some two hours away, the current swirling and racing under the reflective blue light of the moon and the approaching torches.

The grass was wet and the ground muddy. There was now urgency as they pushed and corralled us across the rutted field. I felt a palm hit me firmly between the shoulder blades and I stumbled. The man who pushed me from behind me caught me, throwing me forward again, 'Move, move,' he snarled, his voice staccato and irritated.

The moon was full and the light shone across the river, running fast and silent, swollen by months of rain. In front of us, silhouetted figures crouched beside the outline of a speedboat.

'Get in, get in, quickly, move now,' a gun barrel nudged me.

I climbed into the boat and, turning, took Shirley's hand. The boat was an A23, a simple open, fibreglass boat with a large 75 horsepower engine. I sat with my arms pulling Shirley close to me. The hard, wooden seat was wet from the rain, and we sat shivering, bewildered. Behind us Alanna and Ian were flanked by two of the gang and, in front of us, sat an incongruous pair, one with shaven head, heavily built and with a low-pitched voice. The other was diminutive in an oversized hooded blue sou'wester, and with a shrill excitable voice. He spat some instructions to the boatman who pulled the engine cord, firing it first time. Quickly replacing the engine cover he opened the throttle and the boat surged forward, catching the current. The prow rose, the boat slapping against the small waves, and one of the heavier men climbed across the seats to the front of the boat. Acting as ballast, the boat caught speed and, as it aquaplaned, the engine noise dropped to a steady drone.

We raced by the sleeping communities, illuminated by flickering kerosene lamps from which yellowy reflective fingers reached out across the river to the boat. The breathing of the men was excitable and animal-like as they looked constantly around to see if anyone was making chase. The boatman was clearly proficient, swerving this way and that to avoid the bobbing water bottles that were tied to fishing nets just a few inches beneath the surface. To get the engine snared in one of these would instantly immobilize the boat, a thought that was both hopeful but at the same time may have caused them to act precipitously and at our expense.

Gradually the lights of the villages grew fewer and further apart until we seemed to be racing headlong into utter darkness. I pulled Shirley close to me. She didn't move and looked only forward. There was nothing we could do. After the trauma and shock of our capture there was in fact a strange peace and respite in simply sitting on the boat. The noise of the engine and the wind made speech impossible. The lightness of the boat and its speed made it precarious. Everyone was still each in their own disparate thoughts. Shirley had realized, like me, this was the nightmare scenario. All control and autonomy were gone. This was a new reality and one in which we had no control. Shirley was praying, her words all but lost in the wind. She was committing the situation to God, resolving in her confusion that God still remained sovereign of all. Speaking biblical truth is empowering. Paul, like the psalmist, declared that as he believes, therefore will he speak. There was indeed comfort in affirming the sovereignty of God and our trust in Him even though the heart was weak and faltering.

After perhaps an hour, the smaller of the two men in front, once sure we had left the lights of the last community behind, drew out a large handheld torch and, raising his arm up, used the long piercing beam to navigate off the main river to the left and down a winding tributary. He flickered the light left or right to help direct the boatman. I had a good understanding of the region and tried to follow in my mind the direction of the boat. We must be within half-an-hour or so of the Atlantic where the Niger disgorges its alluvium into the Bite of Benin. This was the empty quarter and the home of so many disenfranchised pirate gangs and militants, secure in the myriad of creeks and mangrove swamps that are impenetrable to the outsider. The rainy season had been long and was drawing to its end. The rivers had long burst their banks and there was no land visible for miles.

As we dropped speed we saw the occasional tiny campfire on a little jetty, with maybe one man, crouching, silhouetted against the flames. They were lookouts guiding us toward our destination. This had obviously been planned well in advance. With each campfire the speed reduced until, coming around a final bend, the engine was cut and we coasted gently toward a thatched hut atop a rickety jetty, from where four or five men came out kneeling to hold the boat tight against the platform. The small man climbed out chatting excitedly and purposefully to the others. Was this the leader? He seemed to have a clear authority despite his diminutive size. He didn't speak to us, or look back, now laughing with an edge of hysteria.

Accompanied by three or four men, the boatman pulled up the engine and standing, used a bamboo pole to punt the boat into the flooded jungle beside the hut. Nothing was said. The canopy of the jungle began to close over us as the boat was coaxed between palm trees and clinging vines, ever deeper and ever darker into the interior. The chattering of the men on the small jetty grew distant. The moon was now obscured by the canopy of trees, though after some minutes light dappled on the floodwater revealing a small bamboo platform just inches above the flood. On top of the pontoon, maybe three metres by four, were two mattresses under two hanging mosquito nets, ghostly and gossamer white.

As the boat was tied against this platform the men jumped out and, scooping water into a bucket, gestured that we should climb out one by one. Having done so, they carefully and gently washed our feet that were coated in mud – it seemed a curious but thoughtful gesture – then pointed that we should get under the mosquito net, Alanna and Ian under the first and Shirley and me under the second. As I stood holding the mosquito net for Shirley, spidery hands ran up my thighs patting the pockets of my cargo pants and then reaching in to pull out my watch, which I had taken off on the boat and secreted away from prying eyes. I felt disgust at such barefaced thievery.

The men re-boarded the boat, reversed and quietly slid away, again the boatman punting silently and another at the front pushing the boat away from creepers and trees, leaving us in this surreal situation, on two mattresses in utter dark, suspended just inches above a flooded jungle, atop some bamboo poles, which were no more than ten feet by eight, open on each side, and the canopy of trees our roof. We were literally floating above water, without reference to anything – a new paradigm – our minds scrambled and confused.

We sat for a moment relieved to be on our own.

The structure had no roof or walls. One mattress had a wooden blanket, the other a sheet. Occasionally a fish would surface by the pontoon with a loud 'plop'. Crickets sounded in the trees, an occasional firefly danced by, and the occasional night bird would shriek in the treetops.

The river had flooded the jungle to a depth of six to eight feet during the rainy season, which had just ended. There was no land for miles, and the topography of the region was lost except to the local indigenes, who could navigate by intuition. We stayed in this limbo for perhaps thirty minutes.

Then silently and unexpectedly, a dugout canoe slowly slid into our clearing.

A quiet voice spoke with reassurance, 'Don't worry, everything will be okay.'

He slowly circled the platform, dipping his oar quietly, repeating the phrase two or three times before once more gliding invisibly away. Though we couldn't see the man, his voice was soft and encouraging. His English was pidgin but clear, and hearing his words gave some comfort – that perhaps all would in fact be well.

Though hostage taking is common in the Niger Delta, most individuals are released in a few days unharmed, on payment of ransom. Universally, foreign hostages are employees of oil companies or ancillary industries. I couldn't, however, get out of my mind a photo of two British hostages held for a number of months, one eventually being released on health grounds and the other many weeks later.

A flurry of thoughts came into our minds. Everyone in the region knew us. This had to be a mistake, and most likely somebody would know somebody, who would know somebody who could clear up the misunderstanding with our captors. Shirley was sure that this would be over very soon.

There was much to be positive about. After all, we work with the very people who did this sort of thing in the past. When we visited Enekorogha many years ago for the first time, to tell how God had wanted us to set up a clinic in their community, the community council and chairman were visibly puzzled and suspicious. We perhaps should have read the clues. They were all inebriated, and the chairman slumped in his chair, his vest emblazoned with the silk-screened words 'NO MONEY, NO FRIEND'.

We had not known that, only a few months earlier, there had been a foreign hostage taken in the community, released only after the army intervened.

Through God's grace and maintaining a steady witness of the gospel, transparency of intent and the relentless delivery of evidenced-based, compassionate health care, it was for our blessing that the poacher eventually turned gamekeeper.

Two years after setting up the clinic, two boats arrived one evening at the community. One of the gang was allegedly ill, and they wanted to find the white men for medical help. The leader of the group was recognized as a known hostage taker and general miscreant. The men of Enekorogha, who considered us to be 'their people', rushed us to a safe house as they sought to round up the kidnappers who had dispersed into the community to look for us. They were eventually caught, their concealed weapons removed; they were beaten and, with the threat of death if they returned, sent on their way. Men who were schoolteachers and community council members then arrived at our accommodation with sports bags full of automatic rifles and handguns, cigarettes and alcohol. One even carried a crossbow. In army fatigues and balaclavas, their bravado fortified by the local Seabreeze gin, they dispersed to the jungle surrounding the house, guarding us all night in case of a further incursion. A team photo shoot was taken the next morning, with suitably serious and menacing expressions of intent. It revealed whole hidden strata to individuals we thought we knew, and a community resolved to come together against a common threat. This really forged a sense of unity and was reinforced by our return a few months later.

In a society where everyone seems related to everyone else and mobile phones are universal it seemed inconceivable that 'our people' would not be quick to respond and sort this mess out.

Then again, the picture of the two British hostages kept coming back to my mind. Reasoning and logic had no place here and we realized as we talked that, as Christians, this was not the time to lean unto our own understanding. Whatever thought gave us comfort, another followed on its heels that caused the heart to race, and fear and anxiety to rise.

I thought of Leo. I knew he would be torn between whether he should stay or take the car back to the airport for his flight home as planned in the morning. Could we perhaps sort this mess out and get back at first light?

My mind wandered to that point when there is a final security check on the tarmac just before boarding the night-flight home; getting through customs and the rigmarole of the baggage checks to get past this final hurdle and the perfunctory frisking, then climbing those steps into the welcoming air-conditioned interior of the A370, bringing with it a sense of unbridled relief. After perhaps forty-five to fifty times running the gauntlet of Port Harcourt departures, reaching your allocated seat never fails to dissipate the stress.

This seemed one million miles away from the nightmare we were now involved in, and the sheer loss of control if thought about for too long engendered absolute panic.

What differentiates a Christian in this situation? Human emotions and reactions to the unknown express our humanity. Fear, anxiety, bewilderment, these are all natural and normal. They are, however, emotions that deny the sovereignty of God and demonstrate a lack of trust and faith, capitulating rather to the dominance of circumstance and evil. We therefore brought the whole situation before God, acknowledging the humanity of our response to the situation but also consciously affirming our trust that God would deliver us and that, like a mustard seed amidst the maelstrom of our emotions, we would place our faith in the promises of God in surrender and submission to His will. This was not a natural thing to do in this situation, emotions and thoughts were racing unchecked. This was an act of intentional faith, of obedience.

As we did this, we felt we had put everything down. There was nothing else to do. There was nothing else to say. There was silence around us – even the fauna of the jungle was ambient and docile. There was no sound of the men and an eerie peace had descended on our tiny clearing. Above, a blue moonlight could be seen through the patchy canopy of the trees. The adrenaline surge like nothing we had ever experienced was now fading and in its place fatigue and total exhaustion brought a deep and almost immediate sleep.

# 3
# EVERYTHING CHANGED

There is often that moment on the waking when, just for a moment you can't remember where you are. Then reality presses in. Shirley opened her eyes. She felt me stir but obviously had been awake for some time. Though still night, the faintest outline of the treetops had begun to stand out against the sky. We could only have been asleep for maybe two hours.

Dawn was creeping over the Niger Delta. In the distance, a deep resounding drum beat out slowly followed by silence, then another three beats, a second or two apart, a pause, then triplets. I felt my pocket and then remembered my watch was gone.

We always had devotions at 7 a.m. At the Mission Shirley and I would try to get up between five and six for a coffee and some time of peace to read the Bible and prepare ourselves for the day at the home-made table. Shirley always sat with her back to the window. I sat opposite her and, nursing a coffee, in reflection would watch dawn creep over the jungle beyond the compound wall.

It must be shortly after five. The jungle drums seemed to welcome the first light of another day. Such drums were common in the region, belonging to fetish shrines in which drums and offerings of alcohol and fruit were made to the riverine deities, part of a pantheon stretching back 2,000 years.

Shirley reached through the mosquito net putting her hand on Alanna's shoulder and whispering, 'Are you okay?'

'Grand,' Alanna replied. It was not convincing.

Alanna looked vulnerable in her shorts and T-shirt. I gave Shirley my T-shirt and Shirley passed her wrap to Alanna to cover her legs. She was obviously relieved.

Ian stirred. Ever conscious of probity, he lay his head to Alanna's feet. In this predicament it looked almost comical. Somewhere unseen but not too far away a rhythmic chopping sound began, as if a tree was being cut down. Some voices sounded, though they were faint and distant. The language was Ijaw, not pidgin English, and the tone was confrontational.

Each of us looked around, taking in with clarity for the first time, the full significance of what had happened the preceding night. My mind raced to the Bougainvillea Hotel where we should now be enjoying a morning of solitude and quiet before the taxi ride to Port Harcourt airport and our flight home. My muscles tensed in frustration and disbelief that we should be in this situation. Noticing this, again Shirley called us to prayer. We sat in a circle, reaching through the mosquito nets to hold one another's hands. Quietly and intentionally we laid the situation before God, lifting our families in prayer and seeking God's mercy for deliverance and freedom.

Our voices were calm and our prayers straightforward, and we reminded ourselves that where two or three are gathered together, there is the promise that Jesus will be present with us in our midst. This gave immediate comfort and unity.

As we opened our eyes, a young man in a blue hoodie and filthy grey shorts came quietly paddling towards the pontoon. His canoe was carved from mango wood. It was split and had been repaired many times with pitch and tin tacked across the repairs.

A new canoe is pale and light apricot in colour, the wood smooth and chisel marks still clear. This one was black, the wood old and rotten. There were three inches of water in the bottom and a cut, plastic bottle served as a makeshift bailer. He tied the canoe to the edge of the pontoon and started bailing the water flinging it over his shoulder.

Shirley looked at him staring back at us with a sullen expression. She lifted her hand and gave him a 'thumbs up' to see if he was friendly.

He hesitantly raised a thumb in reply, unconvincingly.

Shirley mimed drinking from a bottle.

Without acknowledging the request, he pulled the rope and the slipknot gave way. With his paddle, long and hand carved, the blade tapering to a sharp point, he pushed himself back and paddled slowly away towards what may have been a small thatch structure that seemed to poke out from behind a vine fifty to a hundred metres away.

Within minutes he returned with four large bottles of Nigerian drinking water. He handed them to us, his face expressionless, his eyes lifeless.

The water was refreshing. We were dehydrated and almost finished a bottle each. A mosquito net and clean drinking water allayed our two most immediate health concerns. Falciparum malaria is a killer and our immunity was that of a newborn baby. We had no antimalarials, and what would be a two-day fever for an indigene would be for us very possibly fatal. Typhoid and cholera are endemic, so provision of clean drinking water came as a huge relief.

A voice behind us was familiar.

'What would you like to eat? Do you eat monitor lizard?' It was the faceless voice from last night. We turned as a man drew alongside the pontoon in another canoe.

Food security was vital, and we knew bread, nuts and biscuits would be safe.

He nodded. 'Anything else?'

Ian asked for a Bible and some reading glasses. Where would they find these in the middle of the flooded jungle? It seemed a remote hope. The man pointed to some small rucksacks piled on the corner of the pontoon.

'Take anything you want from there,' waving his arm. Beside the rucksacks lay an ancient television, just inches from falling into the water, grey and as deep as it was wide. It was a surreal sight. I crawled out of the net and unzipped a bag. A toilet roll fell out, a toothbrush, T-shirt and some folded shorts.

Shirley waved me back. 'Just leave it and get under the net. Come on, leave it, we don't know whose they are.'

She was right. They were probably the kidnappers' bags. It would be foolish to meddle.

The man re-emerged from the green curtain of vegetation, his canoe low in the water, two bags between his legs. He was about forty years old, thick set and with rather bulging eyeballs and a divergent squint. Which was the dominant eye I should talk to, I puzzled? Maybe his left ...

He handed the bags to Ian and then, with caution and looking around, he placed a silver crucifix into Ian's hand. 'Is this real silver?' he whispered.

Ian turned it over a couple of times. He paused. 'No, I don't think it is,' he said gently, handing it back.

The man tilted his head. 'Okay, no problem.' He paused, stroking the almost imperceptible beard on his chin and, wiping his head, picked up his oar and quietly paddled away.

We were alone.

On the pontoon beside the bags lay a small red, pocket Bible and a pair of reading glasses. It was providential. Ian was delighted and carefully placed the Bible and glasses under the mosquito net near Alanna. He returned to explore the contents of the bag, presenting each item with a sense of elation: Lipton's teabags, a box of sugar cubes, bread, a glass bottle of groundnuts – the top screwed on and fastened with masking tape – and a box of the ubiquitous Cabin biscuits. Cabin biscuits seem unique to

West Africa and are often presented at community gatherings as gestures of welcome and friendship; they are bland, plain biscuits packed in three rows with a rather incongruous cover picture of two American High School students resplendent in mortarboards. The maker's name was Yale, and perhaps this emblem of western success was aspirational in some sense.

The last items in the bag were a green, plastic mug and spoon. Despite the situation, there was much to give thanks for. We again held hands giving thanks to God for this miraculous provision and, more importantly, for the Bible from which we read Psalm 23 and Psalm 46, affirming God's protection in the midst of trial.

As we concluded, the man with a squint returned in the canoe, presenting us with a plastic bottle of very hot water, so much so the plastic had buckled in the heat.

Ian took the bottle and, squatting beside the bags, asked if we wanted some tea or BournVita. It seemed a ludicrous question, to offer a cup of tea in a situation like this and we couldn't help but smile.

Ian, always calm and metered, played up a little the necessity for a good hot drink at a time like this. He was always a wonderful travelling companion, never fazed and always adaptable in any situation he found himself in. Our meeting Ian some five years previously was certainly of God. Whilst searching for an Indian eye-care charity (of the same name) online, the search came up with 'Ian Squire's charity Mission for Vision', just outside London.

It seemed a strange coincidence and, checking his website, I was amazed to discover he was an evangelical Christian taking the gospel across Africa and South America through the vehicle of Eye Care to the most disenfranchised and needy in the remotest of places. Both he and his wife Brigitta undertook remote eye camps to many hundreds of people, restoring sight and preaching the gospel of Jesus Christ. It was clear his business underwrote much of his mission. He was a man of service and self-sacrifice.

My spirit quickened when I read his testimony and I travelled down to meet him.

I found a man serious about God and determined to live out his faith with authenticity and rigour. He had a restlessness and dis-satisfaction with much of the established church, believing that the legalism and tradition had cooled many Christians' walk. It was this sense of frustration that had led Ian to sponsor pastoral teaching to local Pastors by a close friend Alex Tinson, who travelled on many of the camps to teach on the need for sound doctrine where so many leaders of local churches had had such little mentoring. For some time Ian had felt God prompt him to set up eye-care training centres in Congo and the Niger Delta, and he had been out with us annually to set up a training centre at our main clinic base at Enekorogha. This last trip had completed the training of three workers, and the refraction clinic and lens-grinding laboratory were now fully up and running.

A few months earlier Ian had handed over a large Eye Care training facility in Kinshasa to a colleague, feeling it was time to step back. From nothing he had created the only school for optometrists in the entire Congo, a significant achievement, but one he would always credit to God's sustaining hand. This was to be his final trip to the Delta, the training now complete.

The sun was risen and the heat of the day was rising. In less than twelve hours this small pontoon seemed to have everything we would need in the short term. Though our flight would be leaving in a few hours, we felt increasingly that our ordeal would be short-lived. Ian passed the green cup around, but the hot chocolate tasted of plastic and a hot drink seemed to belong to another time and another place, somehow inappropriate in this setting. Moments of elation such as when the food arrived, quickly passed with intrusive thoughts and 'what ifs'.

The practicalities of urinating were discussed, a matter perhaps easier for Ian and me to countenance than Shirley or Alanna. Thankfully for Shirley her African wrap doubled as a makeshift screen to squat behind, but Alanna was resolute.

It had probably only been two hours since dawn had come up, and there was little else to distract us. As we sat on the mattresses, another canoe came by, a small man dipping the long oar into the water and pulling gently, an automatic rifle in his lap and a metal box between his feet. He did not acknowledge us and as he passed by, a small brown dog in the canoe stood up, its paws on the stern of the canoe. It was whining gently. Within thirty seconds the canoe was lost amidst the foliage.

Alanna was sitting up reading the Bible and beside her Ian lay, his hand under his head, announcing that he was tired but, with a little rest, things would seem much better.

Shirley smiled, 'Do you really think a nap is going to change anything? Have you seen where we are? Are you serious?'

Ian smiled back, 'No, if I can just have a little rest, things will be better,' he reaffirmed, playing along with the joke.

'You're the quintessential Englishman, Ian, a nice cup of tea and a wee nap and all will be well!'

We all laughed.

It felt like a bizarre theatre with characters entering stage left to briefly interact and glide off into the wings again. This time the man with the squint returned once more and, without comment and without tying his canoe, he gently laid Ian's guitar on the pontoon before passing onwards and out of sight.

When we were taken, I noticed one of the kidnappers had Ian's guitar case strapped to his back in which he had put my laptop and another belonging to the Mission.

Why would he bring the guitar if it was not for our use, a distraction and comfort? It seemed a very intentional act, indeed thoughtful.

Ian sat up turning the guitar over to check for any damage. It seemed in good order. He climbed from the mattress and sat on the edge of the television. The plastic casing cracked under his weight, and he jumped. The plastic was brittle, perished and weak from the relentless heat of the sun. We smiled, and Ian regained his posture, tuning the guitar by ear.

'Shall we sing something?'

'What can you play?' Shirley asked.

'Only "Amazing Grace", it's the only hymn I can play without my chord sheets.'

How utterly strange it was as we found our pitch and hesitatingly and with deliberation began to sing, focusing with intent on the meaning of every word. Grace so amazing and love so divine, we relished every word, recognizing all the more in our utter helplessness that, despite the appearance of things, we were no longer lost but found and that God's grace would lead us home.

The jungle was silent as we sang. We were alone and sang in worship to our God, to affirm our trust in His unfailing love no matter what the situation. We were sincere, and the words were alive.

This was not a comfortable rendition of a well-loved hymn to encourage, but an act of prayerful worship, where 'Grace, our fears relieved'.

Ian laid the guitar down and, standing, came to sit beside us.

Two cracks pierced the silence, staccato and loud, then a short salvo of automatic fire.

Ian looked ahead expressionless, his eyes empty. He stood motionless, already in the presence of his Saviour, the very one he had been adoring only seconds earlier, worshipping in spirit and in truth. He fell forward, without a sound, into our laps.

Shirley swept his back with her hands; she thought it was an electric shock of some kind, so sudden, unexpected, no cry, no movement.

I grabbed Shirley and Alanna.

'He's been shot, get in the water, quick, don't stand up!'

We rolled across the mattress and into the water beside the pontoon. We held tightly to the middle post, a medium-sized palm tree trunk rammed into the mud of the jungle floor. The water was dark and too deep to stand. Our feet were tangled in twigs and detritus of vegetation. Inches in front and just above us Ian lay silent and still.

All around us was quiet.

We held each other, panting, scarcely able to draw breath with the adrenaline. The shot came from behind Ian and surely there was a gunman moving slowly around to take aim at us. The jungle was thick and it was impossible to see beyond a few feet into the foliage.

Was it a rival gang? Were we here to be killed? Had they realized they had got the wrong people and were now cutting their losses? Thoughts were racing like ticker-tape across the mindscape, fast and furious, chaotic, like a scientist rummaging through papers for a crucially lost equation. It made no sense, we had no frame of reference for this experience, how do we process this?

Should we swim? In which direction? What about the occasional crocodile and snake, the silent canoes of our captors, and which direction was the Mission? It was all too much to process.

Each of us prayed, a pleading, unstructured affirmation of our Lord's sovereignty. It was as if I was in the third person. I admonished myself; here I was maybe seconds from death. What did I actually believe, will I really see Jesus in an instant, then no, why should I die here, unseen, without our sons? I am holding my wife; what can I do to protect her and Alanna? Nothing, no, nothing could be done; it will be the Lord's will, accept, accept that He is sovereign and that His will is all we should seek. I looked at Shirley, deeper in prayer than I was able to manage. She had a quieter, deeper faith, whilst my mind raged with static and with scenarios that screamed through my imagination like a film reel in the hands of a demented projectionist. Then silence and no words came. We held each other. I felt the warmth of Shirley and Alanna, alive and vital – so far, no gunfire. What now?

It was not ours to understand, but our choice to whom to run to. Again, as we had prayed before, even when fear is real and we are helpless and powerless, we still have a choice where we place our faith, in our own devices or intervention from others. It seems that the Holy Spirit was, at the deepest level, telling us to affirm God as our absolute, that in Him we can trust, that He knows the beginning from the end and that all things work together for good to them who love God.

This presupposes of course that we do love God. Again, the turmoil raged but again faith came assertive, remembering the countless promises of God to those who sincerely call upon the name of His Son. The Christian faith is intensely real and practical; we decide each day, each hour, each minute whom we shall follow. There, clutching onto the wooden upright, I decided that for me and my house, my wife and Alanna, we would this day serve the Lord and that, in this situation, simply and intentionally trust Him.

We heard scraping and shuffling on the pontoon. We looked up and two men peered down at us. One was the thin young man who passed by earlier in the canoe with his dog. He was the same man who held the torch the night we were captured. The other was a young man, sneering and bleary eyed.

'You don't say a word' the short man said, his eyes wide and conjunctivae red and injected. He pronounced the words slowly, quietly and deliberately.

He then reached out his arm and, with his accomplice, they pulled each of us from the flood and told us to sit down on the mattress together and not say a word. Ian lay beside us. We could not process this now and locked Ian away in our minds to be able to deal with whatever was to happen next. The brain is consummate at compartmentalizing memories, of hiving off emotional trauma, to lock it down so the rest can function. In the short term this is a survival strategy, but in the long term these emotions need to be rediscovered and processed to prevent a fragmentation of the personality where past hurts and trauma finds no expression and thereby no opportunity to heal. For now, we took Ian into one of those safe places.

As we sat in silence, I looked ahead and made out in the distance the corner of the hut we had seen earlier. It was quickly apparent the short man had fired the shots. He had moved in the direction of the hut with his gun and it was clear that the shots had come from that direction. I tried to fathom why he had done this. Shirley meanwhile was downcast, feeling that now the gang had lost a major bargaining tool and how could they release us when there were now only three.

Once more the man with the squint arrived and circled the pontoon, this time with a sense of malice.

'You people are going to pay, you white people, you pay one billion naira, that's one billion naira, with a "N"' – he reiterated the sum. At almost two and a half million pounds this had to be an opening gambit.

'You call your people and bring the money, you call them.' He dug at the water with his oar and, clearly agitated, paddled away. The atmosphere had abruptly changed with Ian's death.

Almost immediately another canoe arrived with two young men, one who had earlier taken my watch and another one who seemed marginally less intoxicated. They climbed onto the pontoon lithely and silently, then squatted directly in front of us, locking us with their stare.

'Mr David, what is the problem?' The young man pulled hard on a marijuana joint, and then, to heighten its effect, removed the joint and sucked hard between his teeth – a loud hissing sound. He paused, and the vast plume of grey smoke emanated from his mouth, his face disappearing in the haze. As it cleared he swayed a little, sitting atop the television. His friend laughed, licking two rizla papers. He then carefully rolled out some marijuana before rolling it quickly and efficiently between his fingers, lifting it to his lips and, with the one slide across his tongue, it was sealed, lit, and he settled back against the rucksacks, clearly entertained by the level of his friend's intoxication and the ability to make him laugh. They were enjoying the freedom to torment and goad us.

Repeatedly I asked if they would cover Ian, and repeatedly they declined.

These two were highly unpredictable and between hysterical laughing they would grow serious, flinging profanities and obscenities towards Ian and ourselves. One of the men, a youth in filthy fluorescent yellow football shorts, leant on a pump action shotgun, rolling two red cartridges over and over in his left hand.

Shirley told me to be careful what I said. This was sensible, they were high on drugs, adrenaline and the expectation of money, and any extra violence would have added to the thrill. To be as wise as serpents and as gentle as doves was prudent.

'Where are your people?' He leant forward, clearly enjoying the power of sitting a little above us and talking down to us, sitting like caged animals in the mosquito net before him.

'We are missionaries, we don't belong to any company, we are not in oil.' I spoke slowly and deliberately. His English was poor.

'You have taken the wrong people. We work in your communities, everyone knows us. They will be looking for us.'

He leaned back and laughed.

'No, Mr David, they no come here.' He was possibly right.

'You send your people for one beeelion naira.' He wagged his forefinger at me,

'You go call your people.'

'I don't have a phone.'

'You no have phone?'

'No.'

'Then you get one.' It was ludicrous, he seemed surprised that we had no phone. It should not have been so; he had after all raked through my pockets the previous evening.

'Why you here?'

'We are missionaries,' I explained once more. 'I am a doctor. We have a clinic at Enekorogha and Oyangbene. Please, we have no money, you can take us back, this is no good for you or us.'

His sidekick looked almost apologetic – maybe he understood what I was saying.

'We cannot take you back,' he said deliberately.

'How much money have you?'

'One billion is impossible, we are a Christian Mission, we employ your people, we do not make money here.'

He looked disbelievingly at me. A white man not making money from the 'black monkeys'? This was inconceivable. They used the term as they joked derisively toward each other, referencing the 'Oyibo's' (or white man's) torrid past in the region through slavery and, for the past forty years, the trade in oil, and how they thought we perceived them, the Niger Deltans. Their hatred for the generic westerner was long-standing and, given they had benefitted little from the discovery of oil, their resentment was not without cause. It lay at the very root of the conflict and volatility of the Delta, as they sought to voice their grievances through insurgency, hostage-taking and crime. For most of these gangs, including this gang, the politics were in truth a smokescreen.

Uneducated and without opportunity, these men chose crime and violence as a lifestyle, a way to a quick buck.

'How much you pay your people?'

'That depends, senior workers get more, maybe 50,000 naira, juniors 23,000 naira.'

'You have how many workers?'

'Twenty-eight.'

He then dug into every cost of the Mission before firing questions.

'What you pay a month then, total?' He pointed at Ian, giving his threats currency, 'Tell me wrong, I blow your legs off.'

'Let me have your mobile so I can calculate.' Could it be that in his drugged fog he had calculated every sum I had flung out and was trying to catch me out? He looked serious. I fumbled with the keypad of the ancient Nokia and without glasses and moderate astigmatism the numbers were hazy and the numbers appeared double. I was sweating. Shirley and Alanna were silent. As I took my time to calculate the monthly outgoings, the youth in the blue hoodie arrived in his canoe. He climbed silently onto the pontoon and sat expressionless.

'Aah, So'ja,' our interrogator exclaimed, pleased to see him. He was so young, maybe only sixteen or so. He was deferential and, seeing the joints being once more rolled, became a little more animated. He was lifeless from the paralysis of strong marijuana, apathetic and dull.

'How old are you?' one of them said, pointing his cigarette at Alanna.

'Twenty-four.'

The men laughed. 'Then you will be this man's wife.' He laughed and drew the young man to him, as if presenting him. So'ja looked expectant.

The brutality and shock of Ian's death was still static in our minds, adrenaline pumping through our bodies and our pulses racing. It had changed everything, but this new threat took us to a new nadir. The very real scenario of rape and assault was now before us. There was a predatory malignant delight in the men's new-found thirst for intimidation. They had a blood-lust after the killing, that aroused them. Rape was endemic in this region, a crime of consumption of the weak, animalistic and salacious. Here in the fading light of the afternoon, three men loomed over us, delighting in their prey, and a new fear gripped us. What would restrain them? They profaned the dead, were intoxicated with drugs and adrenaline, and we were helpless. The very real imminence of rape wiped the mind of rational thought. It was just white noise and a suspension of time and reference points.

'She's married,' Shirley said with authority. For a moment the man was taken aback, then suspecting this was just to protect her, he waved his hand.

'No matter,' he said, 'she will still be his wife', this time forcefully.

After Ian this seemed to take the day's horror to a new level. As the men became more agitated, joking and pushing each other, Alanna leaned over to Shirley and said, 'If they come for me, don't stop them, they will bring me back. They won't hurt me.'

'Over my dead body,' Shirley retorted, and it would likely be so.

This was pure evil before us, amoral creatures feeding on the stench of blood and fear. There was nothing human logic, reason or petition could change. It was simply as it was. Yet these were humans, overtaken by bloodlust and a spirit of murder. They fed off Ian's death and our fear and powerlessness. These men were consumed by a darkness and evil we had never imagined possible. As Christians we were looking into the heart of darkness, the very antithesis of the nature of God. It then dawned that this was in fact as much a spiritual oppression as it was physical.

Thankfully the marijuana was strong and seemed to ease the increasing tension. They were now drawing heavily, with the secondary whistling intake of air, then, head back, exhaling the plume of sweet, pungent smoke. The eyes were heavy for a moment as the effect hit centrally, then they leaned, their elbows on their knees and head slowly lowering.

The effect was short-lived.

'How much you spend a month? Total.'

I replied, and the answer seemed convincing. It should be, it was true.

'We wan' a beeeelion naira, you understand me?' The word billion was long and attenuated so that we all understood the magnitude. We did.

It was an impasse, and there was no merit in debate.

'Okay, okay, I understand.'

'You call your people for the money.'

So the conversation went round once more.

Then heat was fading and the shadows lengthening. The tension and the events of the day had exhausted us.

A noise sounded behind us and the three youths squatted down grabbing guns.

'Who goes there?'

'Owwoo' a low voice answered. It was a call of recognition, a password of sorts. The speedboat drew to the side of the pontoon, and two men, without comment, started to pack the belongings on the platform. The rucksacks were flung into the boat and the mosquito nets untied, hastily folded and rolled up. They pulled at our mattress for us to get up and pointed to the edge of platform where they told us to sit.

The mosquitoes were becoming very active as the evening light faded. Always we made sure we were indoors between 5 and 9 p.m. when the mosquitoes and the risk of malaria were highest. The conversation had terminated, and we sat slapping and brushing our arms, trying to avoid any bites. Within the hour it was dark and we sat in silence, Ian still beside us. The malignant youths sat with us in silence for perhaps two hours. There seemed nothing else to say.

The speedboat eventually returned, and we were told to get in.

The young man who so played with us all the afternoon, leered at me as I passed him to get on the boat. He paused and looked me in the eye with malice.

'Mr David, be very, very careful ...'

As the boatman pushed away from the platform the very real misery and sadness of leaving Ian could be contained no longer. The pontoon receded as the trees and creepers increasingly obscured our view and it was in almost disbelief that Ian had been taken and that we would see him no more. A godly man, a man committed to serve his God and who had dedicated so many years in bringing Eye Care to the dispossessed, there seemed no logic and no purpose for him to be taken in this way. A loving father, husband, son, brother and dear friend, this act of brutality would be felt by so many. The inevitable question of why God would allow this crossed our minds. The problem for so many unbelievers comes down so often to the question of why God allows suffering. Yet for the Christian, God remains sovereign in a universe where the creation will never fully understand the mind of the Creator. The Bible tells us this and that His ways are not our ways and that His thinking is so much above ours. How can the clay understand the intent of the potter's hands and in what manner he fashions a vessel? When understanding reaches its limit and conjecture steps in we have to return to the Word of God. All things work for good for those who love the Lord. For the nonbeliever this may sound a glib statement, a false comfort without an evidence base, a denial of catastrophe in the light of reality. Shirley, Alanna and I were not fools. In Isaiah God encourages us with the words: 'Come, let us reason together.' All four of us had examined the scriptures, the claims of Christ, in the light of our own existence. Beyond reasonable doubt we had by faith affirmed the veracity of the gospel. We were, like Paul, persuaded by the love and mercy of the Lord Jesus Christ, and this surety gave comfort for where Ian now was, in the presence of his Saviour. For us, however, despite natural human fear, God was still in control.

The boat now turned on the current as we re-entered the larger creek, the engine started and we crossed the swollen river to a small entrance where another tiny rivulet meandered into the forest. To the untrained eye it looked invisible, but the boatman, holding a torch between his teeth, wove his way through the reeds and trees, coaxing the boat with thrusts of the outboard engine as we went deeper into the jungle.

After ten minutes the boat rounded into a clearing where another platform stood in the midst of the flood, this time about five by three metres, with uprights and a thatch roof. There was only one mattress and a mosquito net covering it. The torch beam washed over the mosquito net and we were told to get under it quickly. We were still wet from the floodwaters, and Shirley covered in blood. One of the men noted this, giving her a thick woollen fleece and telling her to cover herself. On the small four-foot-six mattress we held each other tightly, a mixture of sweat and water almost sticking us together as one. I looked out at the faint outline of the jungle canopy against the moonlight and we whispered prayers for safety, for God's will to be done and for His mercy in delivering us. Shirley was so sensitive to all that had gone on, processing it and trying to listen to what our captors were saying. She felt the bamboo poles bend beneath the mattress. Footsteps came over and a figure bent down shining a torchlight. He turned to the other two and said, 'Look, they even hold each other when they are asleep.'

This clearly puzzled them. He returned to the fire they had lit in a metal cauldron.

In the torch beam there was a haze of mosquitoes and the three men whisked T-shirts over their shoulders, scratching their heads and necks and remonstrating. A blue tarpaulin lay beside the mattress and one man rolled himself up in it, kicking and slapping it to disperse the mosquitoes that were trapped against his body. The other two sat beside the iron pot in which the flames were fading. Their shadows danced against the thatch as they quietly discussed who would sleep and who would stay up to guard us.

There was no need; we lay silent, shocked, bewildered and realizing we had no frame of reference for this experience. At times of sudden stress and danger we normally can act upon intuition with fight and flight responses. More complex situations require quick analysis, risk assessment, with a knowledge of available options where a decision is very quickly reached. This was a totally new predicament where we could effect no change. We had no autonomy and no freedom.

We did, however, have a choice, to place our trust in God or to remain passive, simply reacting emotionally to the situation. As a Christian, faith is intentional, believing and hoping in the things that have yet to come to pass and in those things which are as yet unseen. This runs contrary to the senses and to the evidence of our eyes. Yet this is where Christianity transcends the material. For so many, faith remains a cerebral assent to an intellectual theology. Lying exhausted and soaked upon this remote, hidden platform with men of no moral compass and with no way out, an intellectual understanding of the claims of Jesus Christ simply will not do. As Hudson Taylor famously wrote: 'If Christ is not Lord of all then he is not Lord at all.' In our whispered prayer before sleep we conceded that He was sovereign and that in Him we would place our trust.

As the intoxicated youth thrashed around in the tarpaulin beside us, we slept – the removal from all the madness welcome and swift. Sleep was merciful, this second night affording us an escape from the physical reality of the madness before us. In the Delta where electricity is scarce, darkness brings the cessation of activities, day and night establishing a natural cycle of rest and wakefulness – and even a rhythm to the construction of the chapters of this account.

# 4
# THESE THREE REMAIN

There had been a great reluctance this camp, for Shirley in particular, to go. She had suggested staying at home as David's mother was terminal with end-stage cancer and the prognosis was short. In a sense though this was no different to other trips when the thought of the trials ahead was difficult, and many times we had to gird ourselves and go out of obedience. Technically we never had to go at a specific time, as New Foundations' trips have always been essentially ourselves and we have behind us trustees and close friends who advise as we lead. There are a few very close partners: Alex Tinson, who ministers to Pastors in the region and builds up the spiritual health of the team, and of course Ian Squire who brought all his expertise and the blessings of his own ministry, Mission for Vision, in partnership to develop the Eye Care programmes he helped establish with us.

We led all camps as the Spirit led, and we went in a desire to be obedient to His leading. This had cost over the years, as it meant time was taken from home and work, and building up a secure future was secondary to the Mission. It was foolishness in the eyes of the world.

We were later to find that Ian was reluctant to go this time and had even been counselled against it by a friend at church. Conversely, Alanna had prayed a lot before committing to the camp and, even during captivity, acknowledged that despite everything she believed she was meant to be there. She had no doubt whatsoever. Ian was reluctant but came because of the obedience of the call to complete the training schedule of the workers under his care. It was his commitment to serve God that led him in all he did.

For the preceding month Shirley had not only experienced a reluctance to go, but also a withdrawing into a place of quiet, called of the Holy Spirit, a time of reading and prayer, studying the cost that had to be paid by so many Christians around the world in the persecuted church. She had a heavy heart and was seeking God's voice. Increasingly there seemed a widening gulf between living out one's faith in Nigeria where it was deep, proactive and almost tactile, in comparison with a life at home where there didn't seem to be the same reliance on God as we experienced in Africa.

There was an increasing tension between our lives on the mission field and at home, and there was a desire for a deeper walk at home that was difficult to find. Life commitments and simple tasks seemed easy at home, and the ease and comfort made us feel restless for more of God's hand on our lives and a deeper thirst for His reality. Where internet shopping can bring anything the next day, life seemed too settled. Yet all around us the political atmosphere was changing, as tolerance and diversity silenced Bible-believing Christians and street preachers were being arrested for attesting to their faith. Where Christians were being killed daily for refusing to recant their faith in northern Nigeria, Islam had an open door in the U.K., with even the Koran being read before communion in St Mary's Cathedral in Glasgow.[1] We live in a society that had

1. Edinburgh Ahlul Bayt Society: shared Christmas Carol service at St Mary's Cathedral, 2012/14, and the Qu'ran recited at Communion on the 6th January 2017, St Mary's Cathedral, Glasgow. Annual Report, 2016/17.

turned on its Judaeo-Christian heritage, where Christianity was now a minority faith, and tolerance and diversity silenced all voices who dissented from their agendas. G. K. Chesterton's view that 'tolerance was the virtue of those who believed in nothing' was so apposite for our age. There was almost a hopelessness about our society and how we could share our faith in a society that wasn't interested. Life was confusing.

With all this foremost in our minds, we planned the trip. We had deliberately not been for eight months, always telling the team there would come a point where we would not be able to return and that the Mission would have to stand or fall on their witness for the work. It was always to be a Nigerian-led organization. Much of the work in the latter years was to prepare the workers to stand to be missionaries to their own people. There was a heavy burden to train them professionally and spiritually to become mature enough to lead the work without us there.

The culmination of this was the miracle of the provision for the building of the mission station. For ten years we had borrowed houses and had to bring a generator and other equipment. The senior workers had implored us to consider buying land to build our own mission station. This was beyond us, there were simply no funds. Yet following a trip two years earlier and a further remonstration about the need for permanency, funds to build came in to the exact sum in less than twenty-four hours.

One day we had been praying about this request and had shared it with no one. The next day a close friend asked if we had needs in the Mission as he was burdened to help with a capital cost. The same day a Christian colleague who had terminal cancer had heard from God. Meeting to share the Bible and prayer, this time he slid a cheque across the table (it was usually a loaf of home-made bread he gave us). It exactly matched the sum needed to complete the build. Thirty-five thousand pounds raised in less than twenty-four hours. God was confirming the work, and the mission station was completed the same year, a generator house and a four-acre farm to help raise funds for a permanent mission. Committing to the community of Enekorogha was a powerful affirmation to the people and strengthened the relationship to becoming kinsfolk.

We met up with Alanna and Ian at terminal four. Leo was with us too, his first trip to Nigeria. We were struck by how young Alanna looked. She was a trained optometrist, very well qualified, but that was all we knew. She had contacted Ian to join him for a short-term mission, certain of God's leading. She and Ian sat behind us and Ian was deep in conversation about the importance of baptism, citing the baptism of one of our workers the previous trip, and the power of baptism's public proclamation of faith.

During the inflight meal God laid on Shirley's heart to read Revelation chapter three, telling of the church of Sardis, of the things which looked alive but were in fact dying. There was an admonition to strengthen what remains. It was this phrase, 'to strengthen what remains' that hit home to Shirley. After eight months away, it was reasonable to assume this pertained to the work, that there would be much to put in order. It became the focus for the prayer camp, the initial activity of every trip after arriving when, before becoming immersed in the work, we would gather to give thanks and seek God's heart. He always gave us a scripture and a focus for the camp. After years of planning the focus for the camps, we had learnt to listen to the Holy Spirit and tear up any agendas we may have, abandoning the prescriptive folder of 'things to do', that we took on every trip. For many years we simply went, going with certainty but little beyond that. The scripture proved to be very accurate when we arrived, many of the systems we had left in place were flawed, and there were gaping holes in matters of governance and medical care that needed to be addressed; but also the scripture had great relevance for the spiritual side of the camp, to indeed 'strengthen the things that remain'.

During the captivity this took on a very real personal application that we too, personally, had to strengthen the things that remain. As we struggled to pray and seek God about these things, He directed us to 1 Corinthians 13:13, that the three things that abide after all things are gone are faith, hope and love. This focused our prayers as we turned from praying for release to seeking God's will, whatever that may be. He spoke to us corporately and individually about these three aspects of our Christian faith. As we considered these, there emerged clarity.

Each morning when we woke, the over-riding emotion we all shared was hopelessness, but with this scripture we knew it was an area that could be strengthened. After Ian's murder we could not see how the gang could extort money. This hopelessness sought to consume us. Alongside this we knew how remote the region was where we were kept, with no roads, no infrastructure and completely flooded. Since the initial incursion of a gunboat in the first few days and the decoy laid by men that all who were here were fishermen, there seemed no intent to re-explore the area. Whenever we allowed ourselves to think of home, we again felt hopelessness. Our families would have no idea where we were. In the early days our broken thinking led us to believe that our families had moved on and we were forgotten. Though at times we could have escaped, there was no direction we knew to head in, and again there was a hopeless futility and powerlessness.

Like a long-distance runner who comes to physical and mental exhaustion, there has to be a reconfiguring of perception. The verse from 1 Corinthians afforded us the insight that, though the reaction to our situation was entirely normal, it also made us realize that this was a spiritual battle. We had no insight in and of ourselves. On a daily basis we brought it before God that we needed our hope strengthened.

We acknowledged our weakness. 'But he said to me, "My grace is sufficient for you, for my power is made perfect in weakness"' (2 Cor. 12:9). This was the key scripture that we considered daily, that we would receive sufficient grace and strength. Alongside this was 'hope does not put us to shame' (Rom. 5:5). Not only was our hope strengthened, but the focus of our hope became something different. We started to seek the hope of the gospel and all this would mean to us. This was transformational, from hopelessness to hope. This hope that made us not ashamed, made us encourage each other. Being three, there was always two who could encourage the one who was suffering. The men asked how we could laugh and share joy at certain times, how we never expressed anger, and we could tell them of the blessed assurance of our hope in Christ.

Our faith took a battering, but again could not have appreciated without the focus of the scripture. Wrestling with why Ian's life was taken and the kidnap itself was hard. Our faith needed to be strengthened beyond simply hope. It was weak, very weak. There had to be a faith in God in this situation without comprehending the 'why?'

Sometime previously, whilst staying in a bed and breakfast, David was awoken at 3 a.m. This was not a usual occurrence. Deep untroubled sleep is usually the preserve of men, whilst women seem more sensitive to emotional stresses and spiritual nudges. This time there was no clear reason. Sitting up to pray, a voice spoke clearly – perhaps audibly, perhaps not so, it was hard to tell: 'I am sovereign in all things' – and then silence. All spiritual experiences need to be aligned with the Word of God to give them any veracity. This was so. There came peace, silence and then sleep but this statement, given for whatever reason in that little bed and breakfast in March – a small market town near Cambridge – was for now. We shared the truth of this, that indeed God was sovereign of all, of Ian's murder and our captivity. God may not have orchestrated it but sovereignly He allowed it. It gave comfort and reason for our situation, and our faith in Him was strengthened.

As we saw less of the present situation and more of His eternal plan and glory, our faith grew stronger.

At the beginning the love for our families was physically painful. This was the horizon of our love. This was as visceral as the hatred toward the men. We were, however, wrestling with the command to love our enemies; and the accent on these verses grew stronger with our patent inability to deploy them. To bridge the gap, we had to bring it in prayer. Our love for God was taken from a more superficial level to a deeper, sustaining level.

When God arrested us some fifteen years earlier and we rededicated our lives to Him after twenty years ploughing our own furrow, our view of God's love toward us and ours towards Him was enlarged. There was a process of learning that love was not sentimentality, but that true love was challenging, and that true love does not accept anything else but truth. Love is more than flowery words sung over and over in a modern-day chorus. Love has hands and feet and has to be matched in action. At that time it meant putting down everything and acknowledging God as pre-eminent over all things. During that same period we read Isaiah 6, which impacted us as the vision the prophet had of God, that He was high and lifted up, and that He was 'Holy, Holy, Holy'; He is not as many modern churches represent Him, as a best buddy or meal ticket. He is not the servant of our aspirations and desires, but He is the almighty God. He has a plan that will not always mean prosperity or ease of life but does mean a sanctifying process to form us into the image of His Son, Jesus Christ. Therefore His love can be challenging and chastening in equal measure. Our love in return to Him is to learn to submit to this and accept His ways which, as we so often see, are not our ways. Truly this is the life more abundant that He promises. It is not the abundant life of materialist Christianity, but much deeper and rewarding. No matter how often we learn this we have the proclivity to return to fashion the character of God into our own notion.

We must be thankful that He doesn't leave us in this state of broken thinking. The Christian life is not staid, rather it is dynamic. It is radical heart surgery, to replace the heart of stone with a heart of flesh so that it pulses according to God's rhythm and no longer ours. In life we see a faint reflection of this in the way we parent our children. Loving your child does not mean allowing them to do what they want. It certainly does not overlook behaviour that will endanger them. Good parental love challenges and channels the child in the right direction. Hands-off parenting without discipline results in an unruly and unhappy child. The Bible affirms that God like a Father, disciplines those He calls His children (Heb. 12:8). Those are bastards, we read in the King James Bible, who receive no chastening.

Again, upon the mattress, this truth came into sharp focus that we were loved. He was sovereign, and we were in the centre of His will. We asked Him to strengthen our love for Him, that truly we may love Him with all our heart, soul, mind and strength. Importantly, however, is the suffix to this, that we must love one another as we love ourselves.

In prayer, with a new security, knowing we were loved, we were afforded a miraculous transformation that we were able to come to see shoots of love toward our captors, to see them as God saw them. We consciously put down the sin of hatred daily. We were shown not just a grace to endure toward them, but another spiritual transformation took place. We began to experience God's heart toward these men, that He had died for them too. No matter what they had done, He was able and willing to forgive them too. The perceived differences between us and them began to diminish, and we stood on level ground before the cross of Christ.

This experience of how God loves is so intense and at times painful, it takes you out of normal existence to capture a glimpse of heaven and serves to increase a healthy fear of the living God.

This was simply submission to God's will and it took a burden off us. Through submission came blessing. It empowered us to be able to pray for their salvation, genuinely and with some sense of anguish, rather than doing it rote because we saw it as an obligation. They, to a man, had had a miserable life and, without salvation, were heading to a lost eternity.

'To strengthen those things that remain' was answered in a way we could never have expected to see, impacting them and us in equal measure.

As we submitted, we became aware of God's peace; and the enclosure of the mosquito net became a large place as the psalmist writes: 'He brought me out into a broad place; he rescued me, because he delighted in me' (Ps. 18:19). As we did things His way, we felt His pleasure.

# 5
# THE GUNBOAT

The morning reveille of distant drums sounded once more, and again the heart-sinking realization of where we were was accompanied by the dawn's light. A man in grey vest and suit trousers had slept beside us all night. As he sat up I realized he was the man with the squint, who had comforted us with words the first night and brought food and a more threatening presence the next. He seemed to have a natural authority with the younger ones and they referred to him as 'Pastor'. He leaned over, slapping the youth who was rolled up in the blue tarpaulin. As he awoke with a start, throwing the blue plastic from his face, the other two members of the gang laughed.

'Ah, So'ja,' they exclaimed as they sat rolling the first joint of the morning.

Every member of the gang seemed to have a pseudonym, preserving their anonymity and therefore their security. This recalcitrant youth seemed anything but a soldier, but he clearly relished his code name 'So'ja'.

'Ah, Pastor, no vex me now.' He crawled out of his plastic cocoon and drew on the joint offered him from the sullen man who had interrogated us the previous day. He sat, leaning on his shotgun, his yellow football shorts filthy and stained.

He wore them below the waist, homage to 'sagging' and hip-hop stars he would never meet.

The Pastor sat, his left leg outstretched before him, rubbing his ankle and foot. The foot was swollen and wrapped to no effect in a piece of cloth. He pulled his right knee up, cantilevering his weight against it.

'We bless God,' he announced.

I lay, my eyes half shut, surprised at what I had heard. Shirley and Alanna turned to look. The three other men had sat down before him and he, slowly and deliberately, began to sing:

> Good morning Jesus, good morning Lord,
> I know you come from heaven above.
> The Holy Spirit He's on the throne,
> Good morning Jesus, good morning Lord
> Alleluia ...
> Good morning, Jesus good morning Lord,
> I know you come from heaven above ...

The youths seemed to know the chorus and mumbled along, the chorus fading after the second time. It seemed quite incongruous and disturbing. We knew this chorus well and sang it at morning devotions at the mission station most days. It was always accompanied by laughter, loudness and wild gesticulating. After two or three different choruses the Pastor invoked the mercies of God to protect the gang, and, in particular, the leader – or 'General' as he was known – that his enemies should be vanquished, his wife and children blessed, and that all the plans that are meant to bring him harm would come to nothing under the protection of God.

It was puzzling. The singing, the words and the prayers echoed so closely what was expressed in our little mission, and yet the context and intent seemed the very antithesis of all that we understood to be godly.

The Pastor seemed genuine in all he said, seemingly blind to any sense of hypocrisy or irony. Indeed, it was almost tacitly expected that as Christians we would somehow join in with these morning devotions.

As the Grace was said and the little gathering broke up, we sat up beneath the mosquito net and held hands. It was as if the language and expression of our faith had been hijacked and misused. In some sense the language of our prayers seemed sullied, our petitions mocked. As one of the gang was to point out at a later time, 'Satan knows the Bible better than most Christians.'

We sat on our mattress under the mosquito net, exposed on the small open bamboo platform as the sun nudged above the tree line, its glare now beginning to reflect on the floodwaters just inches below us. It was a beautiful sight, and at another time and place people would pay good money for this extreme jungle experience. The beauty, extent and the remoteness of the jungle, paradoxically, created our prison walls. It was all so open, the jungle vistas surrounded us, the platform having no walls, and yet at the same time the sheer density of vegetation was so claustrophobic, creating an impenetrable barrier.

We gave thanks for sleep and waking without sickness. Ian was still heavy on our minds and hearts and we came before God with a simple desire for resolution and release. I rewound the previous day again and again, so bizarre, so brutal, so devastating.

I asked for the tarpaulin to be hung up at the foot of our mattress to give a small one metre barrier from eyes when Shirley or Alanna needed to attend to bodily functions, squatting inches over the floodwaters at the edge of the mattress. The men acquiesced reluctantly. The division gave some semblance of design to the platform, a very sketchy sense of 'us and them' if they were sitting or lying down. To be scrutinized all day, in such close proximity, especially for Alanna, was intimidatory and exhausting, and the banter of the previous day was still frightening, given rape was a tool of dominance and predation in the Delta, and its threat lay ever present in the voracious, lust-filled eyes of the younger men.

The biggest man leant over and spoke for the first time since he had pushed us at gunpoint from the mission station.

'You need to call your people, get the money...' His English was pidgin, rough and loud.

Again, we explained the lack of a phone.

'You get one!', he said with exasperation.

There was nothing to say, we couldn't begin to proffer a solution to this dilemma. His lips were wet with saliva, and he pouted and spat.

The speedboat was heard in the distance, its arrival heralded by the growling of the outboard engine. As it nosed through the reeds into the clearing, we saw the slight man known as the General sitting cross-legged, nursing his AK-47 in his lap. Beside him sat one of his elders, a senior member of the gang, monosyllabic unless intoxicated, again brandishing an automatic machine gun and a doped expression, his eyelids heavy. Twelve bottles of drinking water were heaved onto the platform, a loaf of bread, more ground nuts and, bizarrely, twenty-four toilet rolls. The General nimbly alighted, his sagging jeans black and oily rolled up to the knees, his feet bare. He squatted, leaning on his rifle, and, with animation, began a heated conversation in which it was clear he was talking about Port Harcourt and mobile phones. The conversation was short, and within minutes he had left again, the wake of the accelerating outboard cleansing the water around the platform of detritus and faeces.

A small slight man in his late twenties with shaven head, rolled up black viscose trousers and a tight red elasticated top that seemed to be a woman's blouse, sat silently, watching the exchange.

He positioned himself against an upright of the shack, right against the edge of the platform. He was careful in his speech and did not seem to share in the profligate drinking and drug taking. Unexpectedly he had offered to wash our clothes.

'Why would you do this?' I asked. 'Let me have some soap and I will do it.'

'No,' he smiled, 'it's my job, it's why I am here.' With no change in clothes there seemed little point or opportunity to take advantage of his offer. His manner was gentle in contrast to the others.

'What were they talking about?' I asked quietly.

'They are trying to find a phone which cannot be traced. It is not easy.'

Certainly not, I thought, Port Harcourt was four hours away and untraceable mobile phones are certainly not a high street item and would be both rare and expensive. The big man whom we spoke to earlier was incensed, loud and angry, his speech rapid and explosive. It was clear he was exasperated by the delay but also that the younger man had spoken to us.

He waved his arms in our direction.

'You no friends, you no talk, call your people, get the money, go back to your people, go back to your country, leave Nigeria for us.' He looked out across the waters and berated the younger two beside him.

And so it was for the rest of the day. Waiting, discussing, smoking, drinking, withdrawing and sleeping. The sun rose to its zenith, and the heat and humidity sapped everyone of strength and conversation. We could not stand; they had nowhere to go either.

Mid-afternoon the General returned, this time in an ancient dugout canoe, So'ja paddling at the stern and occasionally stopping to bail the water from the leaking craft. It was another splash from the improvised bailer, a cut water bottle, that alerted the men to their leader's arrival. He alighted and conversation was frenetic. He gesticulated toward the outer creek and, in doing so, we heard a slow rhythmic rumble. It was a navy gunboat, probably only a few hundred feet from the pontoon. Could it manoeuvre down the tiny tributary? We were both fearful and hopeful. Hopeful that they would find us, but afraid of the inevitable gunfire that would ensue and where we stood in all this. Previously, a British hostage had been shot during a botched rescue attempt in the north of the country.[1] Looking around, there was no natural refuge from gunfire.

A brief and animated conversation ensued and the young man with filthy shorts and misplaced bravado lowered himself into the floodwater. He took a shotgun from the pontoon beside him and, holding it aloft, started to wade up the small channel toward the main river and the sound of the gunboat. It looked absurd, a youth in grey vest and shotgun held aloft, wading to take on the might of a military gunboat. It was a lunacy spawned from drugs and deep-held belief in the magical protection of amulets and charms imbued with the strength of their pagan deity, Egbesu.[2]

On the pontoon each member of the gang stood in silence. They reached into the fronds of the roof's thatch and took out narrow strips of white cotton, twisting them into a cord before carefully tying it around their waists. Small shells on metal chains were delicately fastened around the neck, and one or two took a strip of cloth and made a tight bandana around the forehead. Cups of water were placed on the bamboo struts of the floor and with their fingers they flicked drops of earth-coloured water over themselves, silently mouthing a ritual for protection and blessing.

---

1. Chris McManus, who was abducted with an Italian colleague in 2011. He died after a failed SBS mission to rescue him in March 2012.

2. Egbesu is the god of warfare, a cultic deity of the Ijaw tribes of the Niger Delta. The deity purports to have retributive powers and is favoured for many groups who see themselves wronged by the oil politics of the Delta. Charms, protective amulets and rituals play an important role. The god is linked to many marine spirits that are worshipped in the riverine area of the Delta.

More formally these rituals were undertaken at the fetish shrines within communities. It reminded me of the idol keeper at Enekorogha, a giant of a man who kept the village idol, a spirit that belonged to the community that dwelt within his house. Oft times he would seek the idol's protection for militant incursions from Enekorogha fighters into neighbouring communities when perceived wrongs needed to be righted. The idol was housed in a room within the house behind a locked door, putrefying fruit and bread covered in flies on the threshold.

A canoe was pulled alongside, and I was beckoned to get on board quickly. I hesitated, demanding we all went together. The Pastor threw his hand open and gesticulated, 'You must get on, it cannot take three, quickly, the army are near.' Army or navy, it mattered not, both they and us were aware they had massive firepower.

I stepped precariously into the canoe, and the Pastor eased himself in and started to paddle. The young man in the red top told Shirley to get into a second canoe.

'Why should I?' She said. 'Where are you taking us now?'

'Please,' he said clasping his hands almost deferentially and smiling, 'if you do not and they come, we will all be shot.'

Shirley reluctantly agreed and so too did Alanna, following this strange little convoy of canoes moving quietly one behind the other, snaking between the trees toward a speedboat that was moored a hundred metres from the pontoon, hidden by palm leaves and creepers.

We were told to sit in the middle seat. In the prow I noticed the General's boat pilot crouching, cleaning an engine part, his face expressionless and blank. The others called him 'West'. He neither smoked nor drank and barely spoke. It was obvious, however, that he was smart.

Surprisingly the General came last and clambered past me to the front, his hand light on my shoulder as he passed for stability. It felt strange, like a child's, soft and light of pressure.

The Pastor sat at the stern, and West, barefoot and with an agility of a cat, moved to the back of the boat and, pulling a bamboo pole wedged beside the boat, began to punt us through vines and creepers deeper into the jungle, occasionally grunting as he fought to get the boat through the dense foliage.

As the boat passed, the branches sprang back, concealing us. It was depressing.

We reached an impasse between two trees and the boat wedged. West rammed the bamboo into the mud and returned to the prow of the boat. We sat facing the rear, and the Pastor seated beside the outboard engine.

It struck me as ludicrous that in such a determined attempt to hide, they should have left the outboard covered by a bright red T-shirt, stretched over the engine casing. Nobody spoke, but still in the distance the throb of the large diesel motor of the gunboat could be heard. The adrenaline began to ease and we became increasingly aware of our surroundings. Above, a sea eagle wheeled, looking for prey below in the flooded clearings of the jungle. Beside the boat a small microcosm of life could be studied for hours in the entangled roots of a water hyacinth in the nutrient rich waters of the flood. Atop a broad-leafed fern a large and long-legged spider stretched itself across two leaves blending almost imperceptibly with the plant. Below, and in ignorance, a fly alighted.

On the next frond a steady army of soldier ants marched purposefully to and fro, carrying large segments of cut leaves from a neighbouring plant. How unaware they all were of the incursion of this new drama into their world, and how tangential it all seemed to the madness we were now immersed in.

The mosquitoes, however, were certainly interested, and we kept brushing each other's arms and necks when we saw one poised to feed, only too aware that with one bite fatal malaria could ensue.

An hour slid by. The gunboat had passed but they seemed alert to sounds to another side of us, as if perhaps a pincer movement was happening. The sound of the gunboat returned once more. They were obviously alarmed that something could be developing in the surrounding jungle, unseen yet threatening to all. The sense of danger ebbed and flowed, but in time the boat's engine faded as it began a new area to search some way off.

After an hour or so, and apropos of nothing except to break the monotony, the Pastor suggested we eat some bread. He had brought some in a bag for us, hinting that we could be here for a long time. Shirley tore some of the bread off and gave to Alanna and me. She paused and then tore off another piece and turned around, handing it to the General. I turned to watch. He leant forward, his arm extended, and took the bread. He nodded his head in thanks but was caught off guard by this act of kindness. He was clearly hungry.

We ate in silence. The Pastor had declined bread, though had the General not been there he would have certainly taken it. He too was slightly thrown by Shirley's informality with the General.

We drank a little water and again returned to our reverie of silence. Alanna rhythmically scratched the numerous lice bites from the mattress. Her arms and legs were covered in angry red spots.

An arm reached past me and tapped Shirley on the shoulder. She turned. The General held a small bag in one hand and in the other a bottle of Dettol and some cotton wool. He made a pretence of dabbing his arm and pointed again to Alanna. They both thanked him and did as he indicated, turning to hand the Dettol back once complete. He waved his hand indicating we should keep the items; he seemed awkward. We thanked him and again turned back. It was a bizarre act of generosity and empathy, albeit the Dettol and cotton wool were likely proceeds of theft rifled from one of the numerous rucksacks that came and went on the pontoon. Shirley had been prompted by remembering the verses where Paul and Solomon advise that we should feed our enemies, that the coals of shame should spurn our enemies to be merciful and contrite (Rom. 12; Prov. 25). It was a lesson that we were to use many times in the next weeks, to show that we acknowledged the humanity of our captors and that it was the spirit of Christ that was ministering them toward – we hoped – redemption. It was, however, not quite that simple.

Though the General should reciprocate our small act of kindness with another, we were in fact well aware that our positioning and his on the boat made us his human shield should the navy come. He sat behind us with two guns and we sat between him and any possible incursion.

Another silent two hours passed and, it seemed, so too the threat of discovery. The boat was prized from between the trees holding us, and slowly we turned and West punted us back to the pontoon. The young man in the woman's top smiled, he seemed relieved to see us.

The gunboat had passed close to us, yet in this region even a few metres of jungle bush makes anything invisible. We must be less than thirty miles from the mission station yet the topography of the Delta, the latticework of tributaries and creeks, makes any sense of distance unimportant. The delivery of drugs and occasional foray by members of the gang, who came back with charged phones and cigarette papers, meant access to some small community could not be too far away. And yet the Nigerian Navy and the Delta task force could not rely on local knowledge or information to make any sense of where we may be hidden.

The trial of the afternoon had taken a toll on the Pastor. His ankle was paining him, and he nursed it in his hand, the joint swollen, the skin taut and shiny.

I leaned toward him. 'How did you do that?'

It was obvious it was fractured, he could put no weight on it and some days before, he had paddled off to get a local massager – a traditional healer who set bones – to apply poultices and massage. These native healers are considered first line in rural areas where access to modern medicine is scarce, and often there is a spiritual component to the treatment. He returned in worse pain than he had left, the ankle wrapped in a crepe bandage and some red liquid oozing through; at first it looked like blood but he told us it was a chilli poultice. He was in agony with the burning pain. Capsaicin cream is used worldwide for desensitizing nerve pain in certain neuropathies, the active ingredient capsaicin being the ingredient that gives chilli its heat. This uber-variant administered by the local massager had clearly taken the Pastor to the next level.

I reached out of the net and gently held his ankle. Point tenderness over the ankle, malleolus and the swelling gave no doubt it was fractured. He had inverted the foot stepping off a broken roadside en route to the creeks, days before our capture, when he had received the call to come.

'I can fix this if you can get some plaster of Paris bandage.' It was surprising what turns up in some local village stores.

He looked shocked, as did the youth in the red top, who was watching. By now we had renamed this young man 'Abe', as he seemed to use the word a lot, its meaning unclear to us. Possibly it meant something like 'please', but it also had other less savoury connotations, I later learnt.

The Pastor tightened his features, 'Why would you want to do this?' He said with irritation, 'You're our captive.'

'I know, but I can separate what I feel about our kidnap from my desire to help you in your pain.'

He paused then snapped. 'That's enough, we stop the conversation now.'

'Why, Pastor?' Abe asked.

The Pastor turned away. 'Because you are speaking to my soul ...'

The compassion for his plight from his captive had shaken and confused him, maybe even allowed some conviction, I hoped, though my desire to help was simply the empathy of seeing a fellow human in pain when I could do something about it.

It transpired that the Pastor sought permission from the General to go in search of the plaster of Paris. He refused him, and that was that.

That night, Shirley awoke in the early hours, while the final watch of the night poked at the ashes of their fire precariously lit atop the bamboo floor on a sheet of metal. She listened carefully to their conversation which, though in pidgin, was understandable. It turned out that two of the gang had been stopped by the army the previous afternoon. They were paddling on the river, likely as not running an errand. They had been interviewed by soldiers on the gunboats and their story of being fishermen had obviously been believed. As indigenes of the Delta they had presented the story that was plausible and had led the gunboat captain to move on to different tributaries. We were not to hear gunboats again during our time of captivity, a mixed blessing perhaps.

Shirley shared what she had heard and with it came the overwhelming realization that help was not around the corner. To this point, if we were honest, we had been praying what our hearts were pleading for, release and deliverance. At this very point we knew our prayers were those of self-interest and self-determination. We wanted God to work in our way, in our time and for our purposes. Surely this was the very antithesis of real prayer. God had been taking us through daily readings, and at this moment we had been in the book of Hebrews considering how, in chapter 11, so many prayers were answered yet not necessarily to be seen by those who petitioned God for a specific outcome.

The manner in which Ian had been taken from us, abruptly and almost clinically showed us the veneer that existed between us and eternity, and for the Christian the entrance into the immediate presence of God. Though it had only been a few days, today, with this new news, we felt particularly alone. But as we read Hebrews 12:1 that sense of isolation was shattered. For we were indeed surrounded by a cloud of witnesses, not in the sense that some may think, as some sort of spiritual entities, but as just the surety of God's presence in the lives of those who love Him and serve Him, and that He will never leave us. But also, there was a new sense of the witness of others who have gone before, Christians from all backgrounds and situations who were now gathered with the saints in eternity and in the presence of God. This sense of unity gave us great comfort and great hope.

With waking came the burden of all that had happened and the not knowing what lay ahead. We felt the burden of grief for Ian, the anguish of missing family and, in honesty, the outrage, frustration and anger at our captivity. The writer of Hebrews instructs us to lay aside every weight and every sin that so easily besets us. This was such a practical verse, for we immediately recognized that the weights of sadness, grief, frustration and anger were the very things that prevented us from entering into prayer and into the victory for the coming day. We held onto these emotions, these resentments, this sense of injustice, and they prevented us giving thanks in all situations and rejoicing in tribulation, which Paul commands us to do. Just as a runner cannot carry a backpack of stones as he competes, so for us to run our race, these feelings – which in reality are nothing but sin – must be laid down, consciously and intentionally. In the same way, as we forgive those who hurt us, we release them and are no longer encumbered, but instead are free ourselves. This is a very deliberate act and again shows us how practical Christianity is. It is to do with the will and our decision-making. We read Hebrews 12 verses 1 and 2 from this day on. Paul's allusion to the Christian walk being a race was so true. As we lay on the mattress we had no idea how long the race would be. Again we could only take one day at a time, in fact sometimes only a minute or two at a time, consciously bringing under subjection the sheer carnality of our thoughts and emotions and laying them aside. With the weights gone, we were then free to run the race of that day with patience.

# 6

# GRACE

*My grace is sufficient for you, for my power is made perfect in weakness (2 Cor. 12:9).*

Grace became a tangible commodity every day, with size and dimensions. It was something we did not have in and of ourselves but was something that we received, something that was enough for that time. It was never an excess; like manna, it was something we had enough of for each day; we couldn't put it aside or store it for the next onslaught of fear or anger. You had to diligently come every day to receive sufficient for that day or even for that period in that day. It was something which we read about and we understood in part by reading about Paul's experience. It was actually something I learnt experientially in Nigeria some years before, during a difficult period when I was tired and drained and felt I was done with the whole Mission. At that time we were preparing for a large surgical camp in anticipation of twenty-five medics arriving. The community was just not equipped to host such a number, nowhere near enough mattresses, generators or food, even cutlery and accommodation. I was plagued all that week about the eternal value of what we were doing. We knew we were physically helping people, but we had some family issues of our own at home to contend with and I was heavy hearted.

I was plagued with the thought that we had neglected our family prerogatives for this work and that maybe it was all 'in the flesh' and we had lost so much of our own life in these years of travelling to Nigeria to see such little fruit. David had moved jobs to fit in with the work and perhaps this in a perverse way was all self-interest. Every day I woke with a heavy heart thinking it was all a waste of time, and it was another day to get through with massive logistical hurdles. God was going to have to really show me that He was in this and confirm this, but during this time of trouble I was looking at Paul's writing on grace. Several times a day I went to our room to ask for grace, even to speak to people and the endless stream of demands. The grace came minute by minute, day by day, enough to get through and function. This was the first time I learnt of grace as a commodity to appropriate.

The night before the surgical team arrived coming from the north of the country, we called the Pastors we work with to emphasize that the gospel was the centre of this week and that they should look for every opportunity to speak the Word. It all seemed like wading through mud. It was the eleventh hour and I felt no conviction that we were doing anything but providing free health care that was costing us a small fortune.

As the Pastors were leaving, Pastor Ebi paused, then turned, 'You know, preaching the gospel is so easy now, since the arrival of New Foundations. With all this free eye care, people now come to us, yes, and they ask us how they can learn more of the God that we all believe in. We no longer have to go to them, they now come to us.' This was a small aside as he left. I called him back.

'Tell me again!' I said with amazement.

He looked surprised and taken aback, and again slowly told me of this amazing news that people were coming from miles, under conviction and repenting and being saved, but we had not heard any of this.

This eleventh-hour confirmation gave witness of the fruit that was being harvested all around us, and God answered my prayer as I sought His grace to give me strength to endure. The grace was sufficient at the last moment, enough to keep going.

Another time, we were despondent that the clinic seemed so full of seriously sick children. The workers at times seemed disinterested in the work and, despite all our encouragement and training, there was little joy and passion for the work – and this was when we were present. How were things when we were not there, we wondered? We dare not even consider. David was frustrated that for some it seemed like only a job, and the vision for the work had not caught fire in the hearts and again the enemy seemed to be discouraging us on every front. Once more, this had to be taken to God; we were after all reminding ourselves that God had called us here and that His grace should be sufficient. All we can do is break the fallow ground and sow the seed. And yet we are human and need encouragement. We are flesh and blood and want to see some tangible fruit in the work.

Once more at the eleventh hour a man sauntered into the mission house to take tea. He conversed with Victory and the others, sharing a joke and then pointing at us. After a brief exchange and smiling to us, nodding, he left. There was a pause. I asked who he was.

Victory replied, 'He's the grave digger in the children's cemetery, a piece of muddy riverbank where infants are buried in a shallow grave for the floodwaters to carry away in the rainy season. He was telling us that, since you people have come here, he is almost out of a job! And that in previous years he would be burying children every week, but now maybe one or two a year. He's almost lost his job!'

Praise God! What an encouragement; not of course that he should lose his job but that all the work was yielding a harvest of young lives, saved and enabled to grow and develop, who otherwise would have been lost to disease and injury. It was grace, sufficient for the day. It was a struggle, and I studied it and decided it was a commodity I needed.

During the time we were held captive, it reminded us that His grace was available. It was not a theological attribute, not a disconnected experience, not airy-fairy for the few, and not just words. When we tested and tried it, we found it was a reality that in our weakness we received the strength of God. It was real, a visceral transformation. At home in the comforts of our own life we could perhaps persuade ourselves of some form of grace. 'Let us then with confidence draw near to the throne of grace, that we may receive mercy and find grace to help in time of need' (Heb. 4:16). Maybe we had to reach into that font of grace, once, twice, three, four or more times each day. It could be occasioned by any of the three of us reaching the lowest point. In order to enter into the throne of grace you have to actually believe there is a place to enter, of the spiritual realm, where the man of flesh cannot enter. Even on a mattress and prostrate, you can, in the spirit, enter into the presence of God, the throne-room of grace. It is by faith you enter, nothing more. But you also have to accept that biblically you have a right to enter in, entering not in your own righteousness but in the righteousness of Jesus Christ (2 Cor. 5:21). We were the righteousness of God in Christ Jesus. It requires none of the things of the past, we have an instant access. These were things we knew, things we had to grasp, that we may receive grace for grace. Desperate and totally empty, we could come boldly that we may obtain mercy and find grace to help in time of need. This provision of grace was real. At the start it was difficult to come and put everything down but as time went on, we affirmed this act. To hold on with whatever small grain of faith, that God would meet us at that point when we held hands and decided to put everything down and enter in. There was no filter, no eloquent prayer, but a holding of hands and a bringing of our petition before God. And we received His grace, grace that was entirely sufficient for our needs. It was a fact that we, as three different people, had different needs and yet the grace received was sufficient for each of us.

We had such little sleep with all the noise of mobile phones playing music and films, talking, comings and goings, snoring, pidgin conversations of what they were planning for us, and our minds racing, and a real cold, steely fear gripping us in these moments. As dawn came up, the lack of sleep, the burden and weight of all the oppression began to hit. I re-ran the conversations I should have had with our sons. A letter I wanted to have written but hadn't, telling of my faith and what I wished for them, a spiritual will that they should be the beneficiaries of the spiritual truths I had received, scriptures they could look up, a testimony of what was so crucial for our life, the person of Jesus Christ, and the truth of the gospel that I never seemed to be able to get across in a conversation. I had a conviction I should have done this each time we returned, but in the business of our own life I let it go. Even this was challenged by God. All this would be swirling about, laced with exhaustion and lack of sleep.

As the drums began and I woke early, I caught the eye of West, a young man with a beautiful face, but when he turned and looked at us it was with the eye of hatred and malevolence; and there before us was Ian's guitar case, hanging there limp and empty, and the anger arose, a surging wellspring of indignation. The guitar case called to mind Ian, of how much he had given, a mind that was so drawn to the helpless, a life that had been devoted to others, a deep knowledge of God, experience of the world and such devotion to training and such labouring on the mission fields of Africa – and a life taken. These men who had given nothing, who did not care, who had no regard for all he had done. What love he would have shown them and how much he desired that they would know the same Saviour he served and in whose presence he now stood. Grace had to come in such a situation like fresh manna in the desert dew. It was a necessity to find some way to vent this and to take it to God, these sins and weights, for which there was no other outlet. Some water, some nuts and then what, then what? My old self could have erupted and yet we had to keep our testimony, that our flesh could not arise. We must have grace for grace (John 1:16) to enable us to be salt and light, to add savour to our conversation. The transaction was not only for us to keep our testimony but to give currency to what we had to say.

As we gathered ourselves for another day, as morning came, one or more of us was in a dark place. We sat and held hands and sought for grace and the realization that it was our besetting sins that were the obstacles to the free flow of grace. We became aware that these were sins, though it could be reasoned that these were legitimate feelings for people who had murdered our friend and treated us like animals. God showed us these were our sins. We read in Hebrews 12 that these are the sins that so easily beset us. This scripture showed us these were not just legitimate weights but actual hindering sins.

I was once on a Christian counselling course in the south of England and was surprised to hear one of the principal lecturers, whilst teaching on the needs of victims of abuse, talking about seeking God's forgiveness and forgiving the perpetrators of this wickedness. But the lecturer then said she disagreed with this, stating that the victims had in fact every right to feel rage and anger against the perpetrators. It was being taught as a legitimate reaction. But Christ is clear in the Bible that we have no rights to hold on to these feelings; they create a barrier between you and God. The Bible itself says that if you don't forgive then you can't receive forgiveness: 'If you do not forgive others their trespasses, neither will your Father forgive your trespasses' (Matt. 6:15). The lecturer was teaching error to one hundred people, that it was not expected that you should forgive, yet Jesus makes it clear you should.

This conviction grew in us quickly, that unforgiveness was a burden we could not carry. The conscious choice that we made each day was to bring each of these burdening weights before God. Otherwise like a cancer they ate away at you, but we agreed with the Word of God that they were sins that needed to be named and repented of, and to be exchanged for the peace and the grace of God. Initially this was as far as we could go with it. As we experienced this real supernatural transaction, it was sublime in its effects. We progressed on to pray for the men and indeed their families. It was done by faith and obedience, and out of a desperate necessity to have the grace afforded us that was so lacking in our natural state.

As that became our normal pattern of dealing with the day, God continued this process in a way we never could have imagined. He moved us further along His path of grace and we did indeed receive grace for grace. We moved beyond acting out of pure obedience to His Word and precept to a place where He had actually changed our hearts. We began to see the men as He saw them. Jesus Christ in us was loving these men through us, and we experienced a deep compassion for them. It was only later as we looked back that we saw how God had changed our hearts from our initial prayers of 'get us out of here' to the salvation of the men who had taken us. Our prayers were always said out loud, so they could hear that we were praying for them, their families and their salvation. We were praying that they would know forgiveness and His grace in their lives. They had no common grace between them, even pickpocketing each other as they slept. We began to see them through Jesus's eyes, that they could become washed by His blood and in receipt of His grace.

Indeed we realized we were no different to them. We were capable of equally dark and evil attitudes that had become apparent to us in the present situation, that we had such persistent depravity in our hearts, something we would never have learnt in our civilized life back home. When all control is taken out of your own hands and autonomy is lost and distractions are not available, you can clearly see who you really are. Even as blood-washed Christians, we found the biblical truth that 'the heart is deceitful above all things, and desperately sick: who can understand it? I the LORD search the heart, and test the mind, to give every man according to his ways, according to the fruit of his deeds' (Jer. 17:9-10).

We saw that we were simply the same as these men in the eyes of God. Why should you expect these men to be any different? They had never, as far as conversations had made clear, had love in their lives and there was certainly no love in their theology. We had even called them wild beasts and bulls of Bashan between ourselves, as men without conscience and humanity. We had no revelation whatsoever at the outset that these were sought after by their creator God, who loved them and sent His Son for them. The gods they followed were demanding and punitive. Love would never be ascribed to any of them. God had done a work in our hearts and answered a prayer I had been praying for a long time, that I would see people as God saw them and not as I saw them, as 'trees walking' (Mark 8:24). I wanted to see past my understanding, to see people as God saw them. Unless God allowed me to see past the wickedness in men, the depravity evidenced in men's deeds, I would never be able to see people as precious in His sight, for whom He also died. Even witnessing that God died for them too was so vital. I so wanted to see men as God saw them.

I had asked for this revelation for such a long time and now God was working out His purpose for their lives and our lives, answering prayer because the trying of our faith is more precious than gold in His sight. It became more than receiving grace for grace. It was a physical transaction, impossible without the grace of God being poured into us.

We were simply not capable of this. We simply surrendered to God to do this and He poured out His grace through us so that it was nothing of ourselves. It was clear and stark to us, the difference of who we were in the flesh and whom He could make of us if we surrendered. It was like catching a glimpse of the glory of God in this miserable place. As you saw what lived in your own heart, you then saw a flicker of what God could do and was doing, momentarily but profoundly, as we submitted our hearts to Him. We could truly claim that His grace was indeed sufficient.

# 7

# CALL YOUR PEOPLE

The water around the platform was stagnant. Each member of the gang foraged in the stolen rucksacks, and, finding shampoo or soap, took it in turns to paddle from the platform to cleaner water where they washed and shaved. On their return and with their clothes hung up to dry, they again raked in the bags for T-shirts and trousers that might fit them. One lad known as 'Pharaoh', a well-built and muscular young man, returned from his ablutions. Excitable and unpredictable from years of drugs, his husky voice told of a sixty-a-day cigarette habit. Smoking a joint, he danced provocatively and sexually before Alanna and Shirley. He had just put on a clean T-shirt from one of the stolen bags. It was grey with orange and white writing. You couldn't make it up. The screen-printed lettering said, 'Alcatraz, psycho outpatient award'. The irony was lost on him.

Yet beneath the bravado, the machismo and the violence there was something of a child in this young man. A deranged innocence and what would, in the west, likely be a diagnosis of Attention Deficit Disorder that best characterized his inability to be quiet, passive and restrained. There had to be a constant stimulation, be it pharmacological, experiential, physical or emotional. The only time he seemed to rest was when he was totally intoxicated or fatigued. He did not antagonize or take pleasure in intimidation, and though he would certainly have killed on command, there did not seem to emanate the same hostility and cruelty seen in the others.

So the days began to slide. Little by little a fragile routine seemed to become established. The main narrative surrounded the need to locate a phone with embedded software that prevented its location being tracked. Knowing that this was the primary objective gave us hope that things were moving – moving toward contact and negotiation.

The secondary narrative was the day-to-day management of disease avoidance and relationship building with our captors. Overarching all this was the profound loss of Ian and the undercurrent of uncertainty that things could change on a whim or pretext. All the time we were conscious that the army and navy would be now involved, that our families would be imagining all sorts of scenarios, and that the governmental agencies would in some way and somehow be considering their options.

During the day, up to seven of the gang remained on the pontoon. The Pastor, a man in his forties and with a long experience of prison life, had the natural authority and physical strength to keep order among the younger members.

The other senior member, 'Capon', had the brute force and experience to make sure one ear was always on the jungle and suspicious sounds that might herald an incursion or an outside threat. He was a storyteller, brash and coarse. An urban gangster, he held court for hours, regaling the younger members with stories of violence, crime and sexual assault in pidgin English, excitable and explosive, reliving every story, his forehead glistening with sweat, and his hands giving action and accent to every twist and turn of the narrative. He had little time for the Pastor's morning exhortation, adhering instead to fetish ritual and the blessing of amulets he wore around his neck and the strips of linen that he tied around his waist, imbued with a demonic power through ritual and incantation that traditionally would protect even against bullets.

His sparring partner was a languid, soporific man who incessantly smoked marijuana and used the codename 'Wiza', colloquial for 'wise man'. He seemed to be the appointed cook for the gang, and between duties he searched repeatedly for where he had left his Rizla papers and lighter. His stories, like those of Capon, centred around gun crime and misdemeanours. His pidgin English was thick and difficult to understand. He regarded us with a cool indifference, which gradually melted as the weeks passed.

At the foot of our mattress and on the other side of the tarpaulin reaching to waste height, Wiza had a four-foot sheet of roofing zinc, that lay directly on the bamboo poles of the platform. Each morning Pharaoh and So'ja would take a canoe and, with machetes, would cut down small saplings and dead branches of bamboo. Returning to the platform these were to be hacked into smaller pieces for the cooking fire. With each slash of the machete, the whole platform would shudder, the rickety pontoons juddering, making small ripples across the floodwaters.

The staple food was garri[1] which was dipped with the fingers into a thick soup of fish, pepper and palm oil. At night, monitor lizard was butchered and cooked directly over the flames. These large five-foot lizards retreated from the floodwaters into the tree canopies. With a long-barrelled shotgun – similar to a duck gun – and a keen eye, these could be shot from the trees and could provide meat for two or three days. Some days, however, there was no food, but in its place drug runners would bring palm wine, cocaine and marijuana to placate the gang; they were shady characters, including a

---

1. Garri is cassava flour, soaked, ground into a coarse flour, and dried on large steel pans over a fire. It is reconstituted with water and cooked to make eba, a starchy carbohydrate staple food accompanying soups and stews and eaten as a moist dough.

fetish temple priest, who would glide up in a canoe with a delivery. These were clearly people known to the gang and party to what was happening. By now a week had passed and, though we were in a remote area, it was clear there was access to provisions and therefore to people who must have known about our presence but who were too frightened and intimidated to tell the authorities.

So'ja and Pharaoh were the workhorses of the dayshift, Pharaoh twenty-seven and So'ja in his teens. In contrast, the quiet, effete youth in the red top seemed to have an indeterminate role of house boy and cleaner. He chose to interact little with the others, circumspect in his conversation and what he disclosed about himself. One day they pushed him for his name. He refused, and the temperature rose.

'Call me "no name",' he said, laughing softly. He had a very non-confrontational manner, and we noted that he was quick to intervene in arguments, willing both sides to calm down, to see sense and draw back. He was a man who watched and listened and, to this extent, seemed an outsider rather than an insider, without any real advocates in the group. This had its price for, when food was scarce, he was the first to be denied food. We wondered how he had come to be here, what was his pedigree? No-name seemed gentle and with a physique more of an undernourished teenager than dedicated fighter. His right lower leg was deformed and had obviously undergone orthopaedic surgery. He had had internal fixation at a Baptist Hospital in Warri many years previously but had discharged himself prematurely, loading the leg before due time. It was now set at a slightly awkward angle of flexion from the lower tibia, but it didn't seem to hinder him.

He was slight and used his brain and wit as his defences, given he was never going to win any fights. He had a keen eye for escalating temperatures within the group, and with gentle humour, cajoling and pleading, he seemed consummate at cooling rapidly escalating arguments. I had asked him what he sought to gain from this whole venture. He wanted money to go and fight the Russians in Belarus. He had looked at Belarus on the internet in a local cybercafe. It seemed to him the perfect country and becoming a mercenary seemed too good an opportunity to pass up. Unconvinced this wasn't a Walter Mitty moment, one day we understood he may be of such calibre. As Capon recounted another story, No-name suddenly turned and knelt, gazing intently into the forest.

He signalled with his hand for quiet. There was no sound. He looked again and after a few seconds called out, his shotgun primed.

'Who goes there?'

'Owwoo,' came a distant call, maybe a hundred metres away. He had clearly heard an oar dipping into the water, a sound at variance with the jungle calls of birds and insects, and yet imperceptible to the rest. We knew he had form.

So, these early days we watched and listened to our captors as they told their stories, in what they said and did, and in what they left undone. From captors they became people and individual characters. We were sure that like them, we too, though trapped on a mattress, were shifting from prisoners to human beings, whether they liked it or not. To the leader of the gang, however, we were simply cash cows, commodities with a high value.

It was after some days that pressure must have been brought to bear, that necessitated the leader of the gang proving we were still alive and well. Late one afternoon we sat praying, holding hands. He must have arrived by canoe, as we became aware of his presence standing beside us talking quietly to one of the men. We held hands and continued to pray. The sound of the camera clicked several times and it was evident that he was taking photos of us on his phone. Without comment he left.

Throughout the first week, the men sought to test us, provoke us and threaten us. For them, having the white man prisoner was an inversion of the normal – and certainly historical – authority. Their mocking was base and repugnant. Two of the younger men jumped and hollered to imitate monkeys, narrating the absurdity of the 'black monkeys' in the Delta, the words spat with venom and anger. They played out what they thought they were to the white man. It was a sarcastic and nasty play of mock self-deprecation. The oil politics of the Delta had fostered resentment and bitterness in so many, incensed by the lack of return and investment to the region. This drug-fuelled charade conveyed a deep anger at being so duped by the white-owned oil companies. The caricatures of dancing primates were in a sense a parody of their fathers' stupidity and naivety. It was embarrassing, but it would have been foolish to challenge the dancers, high on cocaine and alcohol, just itching to explode in unrestrained fury at these 'Oyibos'.[2]

They wanted us to object and come back at them, they ached for confrontation. This was payback time. This time it was one 'beeelion naira' of payback. From their perspective it was only a phone call away. They were on the verge of the big time.

There was, of course, precedent. Government Ekpemupolo, aka Tompolo, an ex-militia leader in the Niger Delta, seemed to walk with impunity, a warlord of clout and wealth who seemed immune to the Federal Government's efforts to capture him. These men of renown carried cult status for the disenfranchised youth of the Delta, gangsters who thumbed their noses to the establishment and became ever more brazen, pump-primed by stratospheric proceeds from oil bunkering and extortion. Contracts for pipeline protection can earn millions of dollars when the poacher turns gamekeeper. Due diligence when drawing up contracts is farcical. Loyalties, connections and intimidation skews the process, and brokerage will see the flow of wealth continue to those at the top of the pile.

---

2. Oyibo – Nigerian pidgin for 'white man'.

Another militia leader, John Togo, killed by the authorities some years ago, is discussed in similarly reverential terms. These men, hailed as freedom fighters, show that with guts, bravado and force, anyone can acquire wealth and power, though the trail of carnage to get there is brushed aside with indifference. The young men, cradling shotguns, sat on the side of the pontoon, smoking and animatedly sharing apocryphal stories of ever more exaggerated achievements attributed to Tompolo or his like. It was like children in the playground recounting daring exploits of comic book heroes. There was a delusional naivety in the way they spoke, chattering and making the sound of gunfire and explosions to add colour to their tales. These were men but, in a sense, children, unable to critique their world, duped by the allure of quick gain, empty promises of gang leaders and a future where untold wealth and sensuality lay just around the corner.

They seemed to never tire of discussing how Tompolo acquired his gunboats and arms. It was a strange tale in which, following a lucrative pipeline protection contract, he managed to buy a number of gunboats from the Norwegian Government, giving him huge military clout in the inshore waters of the oilfields, and where he could run Global West Vessel Service, which handles maritime security issues for the Nigerian Maritime Administration and Safety Agency, NIMASA. If Tompolo could do this then so could anyone, the young men seemed to reason.

The allure of violence starts early in the Delta. Though communities are remote and isolated, there is often a small cinema hut where violent martial arts films and adult films are screened on a fuzzy television, the distorted sound vying with the Chinese generator going hell for leather in the doorway. Small children can sit for hours watching these films, their young brains saturated at an early age with violent, sexualized scenes from B movies. Mixed with a dysfunctional childhood and family dynamic, the wrong friends and drugs, this malign mixture makes the sort of young men before us, immature, unpredictable and with little, if any, moral compass.

Many patients seen in my own General Practice can appear recalcitrant, difficult and often their own worst enemies, authors of their own disastrous life circumstances and many times chaotic and difficult to help. Yet when I read the psychiatric reports of such 'heartsink' patients admitted following an episode of self-harm or overdose, the life history on the discharge before me is so desperate, so sad and tragic. If anyone was handed the cards some of these patients had carried, abuse, lack of love, alienation and lack of opportunity, it was in human terms alone almost inevitable they should reap the dismal rewards of such a hopeless start in life.

If it was thus in the developed west, then why should it be anything but likely worse in the daunting and challenging environs of the Niger Delta. By God's grace we must see these broken men as just that, sinners and errant by life choices and lack of love and security from childhood.

The light was fading, and the prospect of another night of stress, noise and intimidation looked likely. Above, a distant sound of a helicopter travelled from left to right, another world inside the little cockpit, oil workers shuttling for another shift out on the oil rigs of the offshore platforms. This region of the Delta was definitely 'off limits', lawless and unnavigable. Oil workers spent as little time in the creeks as possible and only travelled with a large army contingent for security. As we lay on our filthy mattress, we were in a parallel world to those Oyibos passing over us.

In the still of the evening the animal-like growl of the General's boat sounded in the distant creek, as it nosed through the water hyacinth to the pontoon. The men rose quickly.

'Alata, alata,' one shouted, kicking awake Wiza who was asleep on the mat.

'Alata' means 'Get ready', and always preceded the General's arrival, the men busying themselves with tidying up, and pointing at us to stay quiet, their fingers to their mouths.

The engine noise grew louder, the pontoon floor was cleared, and the men sat expectantly and with blank expressions, so different to just thirty minutes previously. All the bravado was gone. The General had come. When the engine cut, the boat drew alongside the platform and the General alighted like a cat, silently and sprightly, the boat hardly responding to his jump. He pointed to me and with rapid guttural speech addressed the Pastor. He turned and looked at me then back to the General. Something was afoot, they were obviously discussing me, but in what context it was impossible to know.

It was now almost dark.

The Pastor, now sitting, shuffled back to me on his bottom.

'You are to make the call,' he said.

'Have you a phone?'

'I don't know, you just have to call your people.'

There had been talk of us making a call for some days, but nothing had materialized. It seemed getting an encrypted phone was proving harder than expected and the General was nervy about using a mobile that could be traced. He still carried with him the plastic Ovaltine screw top container, in which he carried his phones and cables. It was dry and floated if dropped, ideal in this environment. The humidity destroyed electrics in no time; it was a clever idea. He seemed, however, to carry no new phone with him.

I cautiously asked the Pastor how I was to call.

'Never mind how,' he said, 'it's time.'

He lifted the corner of the mosquito net and told me to come out. Shirley and Alanna were worried; the thought of leaving them alone on the platform with the men was chilling. We had not been separated at any point, until now.

From such a slight man, the General's voice was surprisingly loud and harsh, rising and falling as he fired salvos of orders and the occasional shrill shriek of laughter. Dutifully, the entourage on the pontoon laughed in unison. Barefooted, and with filthy jeans worn on his haunches, he climbed silently into the boat and beckoned that I should come.

The mosquito net offered an illusion of security, a private space and ours alone. Clambering out I felt vulnerable, the veil of the criss-cross netting gone, the pontoon, the lights of the mobiles and fire had a new sharpness and definition. Wiza threw me orange sou'westers, a jacket and thick, plastic trousers, indicating I should put them on. A makeshift hat was fashioned from a T-shirt, its neck tied in a knot and placed over my head. It was suffocating and hot, but thankfully all understood we had no immunity to mosquitoes.

I sat between two armed men, one, the laconic and bleary-eyed right-hand man to the General, holding a shiny, recently army-issued AK-47 laid across his lap. It had certainly not been issued to him. Stories abounded at night on the pontoon, of ambushes of small army units on the roads, summary killings and stealing of weapons, ammunitions and explosives. The pristine paint suggested this was a recent acquisition. In marked contrast the General sat with his own gun, blackened and the wooden stock shiny through the polish of hands. Taped with blackened medical tape to the black ribbed-curved magazine were two more fully loaded magazines, the copper coating of the top bullet winking as the torch light caught it. Like a musician relishing every nuance and tone of his personal instrument, intuitive in use and individual of sound, likely not reproducible on any other, the General was clearly equally familiar with his gun. He slept with it and dismantled it most nights, rubbing each moving part with oil, sliding the bolt back and forth, examining the gas-outlet chambers to maintain the easy action, a ritual that was comforting and, once done, gratifying and reassuring. The gun gave the small man gravitas and presence. The two men's proximity was oppressive.

The boat turned, and we slowly made our way back to the main creek. Would Shirley and Alanna be alright? I fought back the panic, knowing I was powerless whether with them or apart. Whom was I to phone? No one had said. In these days of mobiles, I had no numbers to mind, all on speed dial. Only one number I knew, Mike, our stalwart trustee in Bury St Edmunds. I repeated his number to myself again and again. After a few minutes I faltered, terrified that I had created a new number in my mind, the anxiety clouding my thinking.

As we entered the larger creek a breeze caught my wet skin, cooling and wonderful to the feel. On the pontoon the trees shielded us from any winds, and the sweat never evaporated to cool in the high humidity.

Within a few minutes the engine cut and we silently docked against a rickety jetty. It must be on the main creek as the light, night breeze blew across my sweltering brow. I was helped to stand and climbed precariously onto the tiny jetty. The General had attached his phone to a pole by string and he plugged his ear phones in, giving me one and he taking the other so he could listen in.

'Call!' he snapped.

I typed in Mike's number. I envisaged him at home with Anne in suburban Bury St Edmunds, likely finishing supper. I froze, for he was often out at the church or homeless outreach. Would he answer? Just as I pressed the last key the General sprang and cut the call, storing of course the number I had dialled. He took the phone and dialled another number, then handed it to me and pressed the earpiece against his ear looking down at the ground intently.

A Nigerian voice answered, soft, chocolatey and rich, with a good command of English. He had money, I thought, and authority.

'To whom am I speaking?' he asked.

I was taken aback. Was this a game?

'Doctor David Donovan.' I answered, slowly and deliberately.

He proceeded to ask of each of us our names and addresses. The General lifted his head and now watched me intently. I knew his mind. I gave the names of all of us, including Ian, without hesitation or any suggestion that anything was amiss.

The air was thick with mosquitoes. As I spoke, I felt the lightest of touches brushing my bare feet and ankles and then moving up to gently rub my neck and ears, back and forward again and again. The General had one of the appointed 'elders' behind me, constantly checking no mosquito came near me. Acute malaria would undermine everything. The gentleness of his touch was quite unsettling given the brutality of how he had shoved us the night we had been taken.

As I completed the call, I tried to tell of how hard it would be to gather funds. Too late, the General reached across and cut the call.

My spirit plunged; there was so much to say, so much these men didn't understand about transferring money internationally. They seemed to think you could simply fly in with a holdall of currency. They were out of their league. I was frustrated and angry as they shoved me to get back to the boat.

The boat turned around on the current and the engine started, as we headed back across to the almost invisible entrance to the pontoon some four hundred yards into the flooded jungle. I sat confused and powerless. I had nothing to tell Shirley and Alanna, nothing to give hope or suggest progress. I had simply given our names to some intermediary. Who was he and was he competent or to be trusted to do anything?

A flicker of light danced from the blackness as we neared the pontoon. A fire had been started on the metal sheet for cooking monitor lizard. It all looked so hopeless and there seemed to be no plan. This was a gang out of their depth and out of control, and we were part of this madness. Again, it was groundhog day on the pontoon.

Disconsolate, I climbed out of the sticky filthy trousers and crawled under the net. Shirley and Alanna looked expectantly at me. I realized some of the men on the pontoon were also trying to read my body language. Clearly they had no more idea than we did.

Alanna and Shirley assumed they would be going with me too, preferring to risk the mosquitoes than staying with these men alone. No-name tried to comfort them, saying it would be all okay, and it was a good thing I was getting to make the call. They had thoughts of my being shot and having to survive on their own. Why wouldn't they, given they had shot Ian, they argued? With one of the party dead, we had significantly lost our value. Who was going to pay a ransom, how would they explain Ian's death?

Shirley thought we were more of a liability than a commodity at this point. Once again Alanna turned to our only source of hope and comfort, and we prayed. We prayed for safety, but over and above this - as God had been teaching us - for His will to be done. We placed our petitions of safety and rescue whilst acceding that it must be God's will ultimately that was done. This gave both Alanna and Shirley a focus and immense comfort during my absence. As they sat in the dark holding hands, Shirley thanked God for Alanna and the biblical reminder that where two or three are gathered together, there is God in the midst of our prayers. We entered into a different place as we prayed, no longer aware of our dark and frightening surroundings, no longer gripped with the fear of being with these men alone. As Shirley confided, 'We were fully engaged in the process of lifting our vision beyond what we could feel, hear or perceive.'

As I climbed under the mosquito net, we tucked it in and felt a sense of relief and curious sense of safety. It was like a hospital curtain around a bed where those within feel no conversation penetrates and privacy is complete. Like baby birds in a nest, Shirley and Alanna eagerly waited to be fed some new information that would give a thread of hope we could hold on to. Whom had I spoken to, what had I said, did I manage to tell Mike of our ordeal? Was the army looking for us, was the U.K. Foreign Office intervening on our behalf, were our sons and family aware of our situation? It was with heavy heart that I gave what little report I had, from which to prognosticate was impossible.

We were left with an uneasy disappointment at the fruitless phone call. Alanna was visibly upset at this point. And again, we placed everything down and sought the grace and comfort of God. With intent but with difficulty, we were able to put everything aside and lay down to sleep. Alanna was first to fall asleep. She had an uncanny ability to sleep at any point, and I too found sleep. Shirley as always lay awake, straining to make sense of the conversations in pidgin English until eventually sleep released her.

Somehow, we had been afforded the gift of sleep. Our mattress was only four foot six and was our home for twenty-two days. We were not allowed to leave it, and sleep was a blessed release from the whole situation. Preparations for sleep were precise. We tightened the mosquito net and wedged empty water bottles between the net and the mattress, so the net didn't touch our bare arms and legs. One mosquito bite could prove fatal without prophylaxis. We turned in unison on the small mattress, at times wrapping our arms around each other when the situation became too much. The mattress was sagging over bamboo poles that had worked apart, and in places there was nothing between us and the water. We plugged any small gaps with toilet paper. At night the pontoon became a spider's web of criss-crossing strings holding up mosquito nets, phones tied to twine from the crossbars of the structure. As guard duties changed every two hours, men were constantly waking or trying to get back to sleep. Most were intoxicated and clumsy, occasionally falling onto us as they tripped over unseen hazards and became entangled in the zig-zag lines of string and twine. Our mosquito net had some holes, and each morning we unpicked some thread to pull the torn net into a little knot and tie it off. It was a crucial and ever-increasing task.

For our captors, however, night was a time of regimented sentry duty. In pairs and armed with grenades and shotguns, they silently pulled a dugout canoe to where our little tributary met the bigger creek and where army gunboats periodically patrolled in a haphazard search for clues of where we had been hidden in the vast flooded jungle. They sat for some hours, smoking marijuana, before returning for a change in shift.

Some time in the early hours we were brutally pulled from sleep by the sound of someone being lashed with what we later found out to be the flat edge of a machete. Fifty lashes were the predetermined punishment in what was an unwritten rule book for various breaches of discipline, from fines to death by shooting. In that hinterland between waking and sleeping, Alanna assimilated the sounds as her own legs being lashed, terrifying if only momentarily.

It was a horror to hear the repeated flogging of an adult, a well-built man, having removed his trousers, laying down before the others and, without remonstrating, submitting silently to the punishment. It was dehumanizing, and the next day the small pontoon hung heavy with a cold and heavy atmosphere. The General had administered the lashing with fury and had left before dawn.

This added a new and sinister dimension to the leader known as the General. He had silently returned that night by canoe, testing the security, and found a guard asleep, doped in a fog of marijuana. He could come at any time, and the men for the next few days lived in a heightened sense of fear and anxiety.

When talking about him among themselves, they often referred to him as 'master'. It became clear that most of the gang had undergone rites, to sell themselves into bondage to this man as part of their following of Egbesu, a pagan West African god of war who, they believed, would protect them from bullets and death. This twenty-eight-year-old man was in every sense therefore their master. It put us in mind of the biblical verse: '... For whatever overcomes a person, to that he is enslaved.' (2 Pet. 2:19)

During the next day as they discussed what happened and referring to 'master', we were troubled to see how fearful they were of this man. How truly they had given over all their rights. Whether they lived or died, they were in his keep. It moved and stirred something in us, of compassion and outrage that here in the twenty-first century they were calling another man 'master'. We were stirred by the Holy Spirit to challenge them.

'You should call no man "master",' Shirley gently, but affirmatively, interjected.

After a pause and some surprise, they came back with a question, 'Why do you say that?'

We were then able to expound on the scripture in Matthew 23:10, that 'neither be called instructors, for you have one instructor, the Christ'. It gave us a window to tell of the mercy of Jesus, and His offer for all men to be free. For at least two of the gang this seemed to be received.

# 8

# TRUTH

*I am the way, and the truth, and the life.*
*(John 14:6)*

What is truth? In our post-modern world we are told there
are no absolutes anymore. Even the obvious 2+2 = 4 is no
longer the case under the common core of the American
Educational system.[1]

Relativism is the byword of our age. Without absolutes
people have no anchor, and truth is what you want it to be. Sadly
in Christendom, this philosophy has permeated theology, and
the Bible is no longer held as the standard of truth. While
many in the emergent church movement pick apart the Bible,
creating a theology based on feeling and experience, many
Christians are left adrift in a sea of confusion. So when your

---

1. 'Mathematically-proficient students start by explaining to themselves the
meaning of a problem and looking for entry points to its solution. They analyze
givens, constraints, relationships, and goals. They make conjectures about the
form and meaning of the solution and plan a solution pathway rather than simply
jumping into a solution attempt. They consider analogous problems and try
special cases and simpler forms of the original problem in order to gain insight into
its solution.' – 'Common Core State Standards Initiative' (U.S.A.). This model
redefines the pathways to solutions along more reasoned and analogous lines,
opening other solutions to previously held absolutes.

life is threatened or your status quo is overturned, what can you rely upon?

When your own ideas, your feelings and emotional experiences fail to equip you, the words of Jesus Christ ring true.

Truth is a person, it is the person of Jesus Christ.

Jesus stated, 'I am the truth.' He is also the Word made flesh (John 1:14). 'The Word' in this scripture is a title for the Lord Jesus Christ, coming from the Greek word logos. Logos is also the written Word of God, the Bible, the foundation of our faith.

Since we rededicated our lives to God in 2003, we turned to the Bible, with a serious search for who God was and how He wanted us to live. It was extraordinary to look back over years as a Christian, how infrequently we had been encouraged to read the Bible. It was just soundbites and snatches of sermons in house groups. In our own experience we had found this emerging philosophy in church to be shallow and unsustaining. We often experienced it as having received fast food, but remaining hungry, living on junk food but devoid of nourishment. It was only when we turned to the Bible to search for a direction of how to live, that we truly found it to be the Word of God. It was during this time we read 2 Timothy 3:16 which clearly tells us that 'all scripture is breathed out by God and profitable for teaching, for reproof, for correction, and for training in righteousness.' It was the 'new foundation' on which we rebuilt our life, and our Mission.

During fourteen years working in the Niger Delta we were confronted by many issues and problems that we didn't have the answer for. The region is replete with failed initiatives and broken testimonies of Christian endeavour. There is no human wisdom and generic answer for the tortuous issues of corruption, greed and exploitation, although for decades men have tried with human ingenuity, only to fail and withdraw.

We saw this and realized that we had the answer in our hand; it was to the pages of the Bible that we turned. The verse from Timothy assured us that the Bible could provide everything that we needed to 'be equipped for every good work' (2 Tim. 3:17). Issues of theft, immorality, of lack of probity in the work, lying and manipulation; to human thinking, all looked impossible to sort out. This was made harder by the clash of bringing our white culture, with all its baggage, into another culture, each with their own very different norms and accepted forms of behaviour. It was a minefield, until we sat our workers down and stated that it was neither a black nor a white issue. It was a matter of lining up any contention with what the Bible says. We put ourselves and the work under the authority of scripture. This avoided personalizing anything and any attempt at coercion, where there was always the excuse that 'this is how things are always done here'. We gave no quarter to cultural pressures but came under complete submission to what God said in His Word, meeting together on level ground before the cross.

The Bible was utterly to be relied upon, and we shared our dependency. The Bible became the impartial and gentle admonisher of our actions as our workers saw that we submitted ourselves with the same rigour. 'Jesus Christ is the same yesterday and today and forever' (Heb. 13:8), and His Word remains unchanging.

Ian left us the greatest gift when he asked for a Bible. At the time he asked for it, we thought we would be out in a matter of days. This was not to be the case, and the Bible became crucial. Initially, we read the Bible together to give a focus and to seek comfort. Our thinking was entirely upside down since seeing Ian shot. There were elements of shock and disassociation. We disciplined ourselves to read it every day and, in doing so, something quite miraculous occurred.

We were literally being washed in the Word and as we were washed, so the confusion of the trauma began to clear. This is something we could not have foreseen and barely could have wished for, but the power of God's Word began to heal our minds.

John 8:32 says: 'You will know the truth, and the truth will set you free.' We were being freed by the truth of God's Word. It didn't matter which part of the Bible we were reading, the truth of the written Word of God was setting our minds free.

As Jesus Himself prayed in John 17:17, 'Sanctify them in the truth; your word is truth.' The disciples were sanctified by the truth of the Word and we were in receipt of the same. As this process continued, our minds cleared and our focus became directed by God and not ourselves.

Many parts of the Bible we read spoke directly into our situation, and we began to apply the Word of God in our prayer and actions. In Matthew 5:44 Jesus taught: 'Love your enemies and pray for those who persecute you.' Our prayers changed, and we began to pray for our captors out loud every day, that God would bless them and forgive them, and that He would enable us to forgive them fully and bless them. We prayed for their wives and children. All these prayers our captors heard. Our hearts toward them began to change and in some, their attitude toward us softened. What appeared ludicrous to a human mind, to forgive those who were persecuting us and seeking to harm us, was God's truth and way of dealing with this situation, and when we bowed our knee to His Word and applied it regardless of how we felt, the truth of His Word brought about fruit and peace.

In Romans 12:20 Paul states: 'If your enemy is hungry, feed him; if he is thirsty, give him something to drink; for by so doing you will heap burning coals on his head.' Again, we applied this literally. We shared what meagre rations of bread we had. A couple of the captors had evidently not eaten. As we struggled to give away what little food we had, reason told us this was a bad idea, but the Word of God and the leading of the Holy Spirit encouraged us to do so. We witnessed a staggering effect that this was to have.

One of them, No-name, the quieter of the young men, was quizzical. 'Why would you do this? Why would you give us your bread?'

We were able to witness to how our God teaches us to act in a given situation and directly impact the lives of some of the captors, in a group where there was no honour amongst themselves. It said more than a hundred sermons could do. It cut through and witnessed to them the saving grace of Jesus Christ, as we explained the reasons for giving the food. We held no anger and told of the God who loved them. We had it strongly impressed upon us that for most this would be the last and, indeed, only opportunity they would have to hear the gospel in its entirety. This was to prove unnervingly accurate.

For others in the group, the offer of bread had a totally different effect. For Capon and the boy with filthy shorts in particular, it was as if we had a loaded gun pointed at them. They physically backed away, their hands raised in the air, shouting, 'No, no, no!' in exclamation and horror.

The contrast between these two reactions was staggering. Those who were willing to accept from the hand of God and those who were not. Later it proved that those who received the bread, were to also receive the gospel. From that point on, those who refused the bread, instead of being in our face and goading us, backed off from using us as sport. This made things more palatable.

The truth of God's Word had real power, power we could not anticipate. In our own culture we live in a relatively peaceful society. In our life at home we did not encounter enemies like this and therefore had not been tested in how we would react. We live in a relatively polite society. We do not have a gun pointed in our face. It's not so stark, not so obvious. We learnt, in a way we would never have known at home, the power and truth of God's Word when directly applied and without compromise.

We were reminded of an earlier time at Obeniama, some years previously, where we were holding a cataract camp. A Nigerian ophthalmologist had joined us to operate on fifty patients screened at remote communities. We had set up the surgical theatre in a politician's family compound. The patients were prepped, and we had four large barrels of diesel to run the generator for the team, the surgical microscope and the floodlights to light the compound. Everything was ready and the operations were due to start early the next morning.

We were sitting down with the team to eat as night fell when we were plunged into darkness. The generator had fallen silent. The compound was pitch black and people started to call out and were running around, their torches and mobile phones flitting about like fireflies. The fans were still and the temperature in the house soared. Robin, an old friend, and David went out to investigate. The youth in charge of the generator stood mute. He gestured to the barrels, they were all empty.

Then the truth dawned. The community had been partying solidly for the previous three days and it was now clear where the power for the music, lights and general mayhem had come from. We could see no way to start the surgery the next day without power. This was a remote community and there was no access to fuel. Such callous selfishness beggared belief. We were frustrated and incensed. We remonstrated to the community secretary who seemed totally indifferent to the whole situation, and that the blind should suffer for the sake of a drunken party. It was pointless, but we didn't want to lose our testimony as tempers were rising.

We returned to the house and sat down to complete our meal. We thought there was no option but to leave the next day. We decided to put down the anger and frustration, and to pray. We sat in darkness at the table. We gave thanks for our food and prayed according to Ephesians 6 that, having done all we could do, we would 'stand', leaving the situation in God's hands. We gave thanks for His will in this situation. We didn't want to leave and for the patients to be disappointed, and indeed to have a broken testimony. We stated this to God, that unless He intervened sovereignly, we would have no option but to leave the next day. The surgical microscope could not operate without power. We had faith that in some way, somehow, someone may, the next day, bring some diesel, no matter how limited.

In the time it took to say His own words back to Him from Ephesians 6, 'Having done all, we shall stand', the lights came on, and full power was restored. To this day we don't know where the diesel came from, but the barrels were full and the camp proceeded as planned, and the surgeries were all completed. It stunned us, defied logic and was miraculous.

It was one of the first times we saw the Word of God powerfully applied, and the camp was joyful and exuberant, with so many witnessing what God had done. It defied our analysis; we had seen the barrels empty, and yet within minutes they were full.

Throughout the twenty-two days of captivity the Bible was our plumb-line. It was our absolute, against which everything else would be judged. It was also our guide. Through the challenges that came daily, we found our focus, comfort and direction from the Bible. We witnessed it to be as it is written, sharper than any two-edged sword. It also sustained and strengthened us, building us up in our faith, where we no longer cowered from our captors, but began to challenge their thinking and beliefs with boldness.

At times the men used us as a sport, goading and tormenting us. We told them we were freer than they, though we were their captives. When they asked us, 'How this could be so?', we were able to explain it from the truth of God's Word, that 'if the Son sets you free, you will be free indeed' (John 8:36). This was to have a dramatic effect and opened up many conversations, the Word of God cutting through their defences in a way impossible using our own words.

Hearing the men calling the General 'master' and witnessing the fear and deference they held toward this young man who held such power over them, we again had to speak out. We told them they should call no man master. They looked puzzled and ignored the statement, but some time later, No-name came back to us asking what our comment meant. Again, this gave us an open door to tell of the Christ we served. And again the Word of God cut through to the heart of one man, and he was visibly moved when we explained there was only one master and he was a servant king who came to serve and not to be served. He laid down His life for us, not as the General was expecting them to lay down their lives for him. Logic and reasoned argument made no headway with the men; it only antagonized them. The only thing that arrested them, drawing their attention, was the Word of God spoken and acted upon.

# 9
# THE 'ASSET'

Episodically a mighty crash could be heard in the surrounding jungle. Distances are hard to gauge, but one time the air reverberated with the intensity of the sound. I asked the Pastor what these were, and without hesitation he said it was palm trees being felled and falling into the water. Without the preceding roar of chainsaws this was patent nonsense. Pharaoh later confided that other members of the gang in different locations were testing explosives and grenades for blowing up pipelines. This made sense as on occasions, home-made grenades, the size of oranges, were stored on the pontoon, explosives wrapped in tight black plastic bags with a fuse like the stem of an apple. For reasons better known to the gang, these were often stored two at a time inside trainers. It was a miracle the gang had not blown themselves up. These grenades were left in full sunlight near an open fire. West and So'ja would pump outboard fuel while smoking a cigarette, and shotgun cartridges were often left near the fire, where sparks would rise and settle from the crackling wood soaked in kerosene to ensure even the dampest branches would light.

From within our mosquito net we had time to study our captors. Though they could exhibit malevolence and cruelty quite beyond imagination, in the spaces between, there was a brokenness and dysfunction that demanded scrutiny.

The Pastor, an older man, cooked for us. He was well built, and he knew how to handle himself. He had spent eleven years in jail for a crime which he remained circumspect about and vigorously denied. During his imprisonment he had been introduced to the Bible and had acquired some sort of faith. It seemed entirely congruent to him to hold us hostage and profane, and yet openly pray each morning. It was not a faith we recognized. He claimed to pray to the same god for the ransom to be paid, the enemies of the gang to be crushed and divine protection for the General and all the gang members. Bible texts were twisted and contorted for his own ends, yet he saw the God we prayed to and his as one and the same. Prayers were said each morning for the kidnappers' prosperity, for foes to be vanquished and joy to be present in the camp. To our sadness he was making converts as described in Matthew 23:15 that were 'twice as much a child of hell'. He had inoculated them with enough Christian jargon to make some of them at least believe that they would make heaven and that they were in right standing with God, despite the mass of evidence against this. It was extraordinary to see this verse played out before us. What Jesus had accused the Pharisees of was replayed here in the Delta – young men, rapists and violent gang members deluded that they were Christians.

We knew words would not be sufficient to share our faith in this situation and indeed, this was a truth known for many years. The detritus of Christian Prosperity teaching and the malign mixture of fetish beliefs and the Bible, plaited and twisted together in this region, had hidden the gospel in a toxic mixture of heresy and half-truths.

Living on this small pontoon in the flooded jungle, this dilemma was brought into a sharper focus.

We had now been in captivity twelve days. Two days had elapsed since I had spoken to the Nigerian on the phone. He had told me he worked for the Nigerian security service, but other than this he had given no indication that help was on its way. Six days earlier the General had taken our photo.

During the afternoons, when the more excitable men were either in a drug induced stupor or had paddled into the bush for firewood, there was the opportunity to gently elicit what information we could from the Pastor or No-name. I was curious about the photos and who they had been shown to. I had assumed it was the authorities.

'No, it's for the community gang leaders,' said the Pastor. 'They want to know you are alive.'

The Delta is replete with criminal gangs, some, though few, politically motivated, but in the main opportunistic criminals. Movement in the Delta, especially in this remote region, is by boat and it's hard to manoeuvre and see all without some support and security from contacts in other communities. It transpired that the General had assumed support from many neighbouring gangs, coerced either by threats or payment to collude with his movements. We were astonished to learn that, universally, these gangs had refused to co-operate, telling him that he should not have taken us as we were missionaries to their people. There are of course bad eggs in every community but those in positions of power had felt he had crossed the line. They demanded to know we were alive. Furthermore, we learnt that the people at Enekorogha were incensed and had taken our abduction both seriously and personally. The photos, it turned out, had bought the General some time, and had quietened voices who had wanted to actively pursue him. We thanked God for this testimony of the work and that God had restrained others from colluding with the gang.

I thanked the Pastor and we rejoiced at this news. He sat looking at us and then quietly said, 'If it was in my power to help you, I would.'

He looked awkward for a second or two and turned away. With no capacity to change anything about our situation, these small encouragements lifted our spirits and we turned to prayer to give thanks to God for each small mercy that made the situation a little more bearable.

The Niger Delta is not a unified tribal region, in dialect, religion or character. Boundaries and allegiances are well demarcated, and transgression of either reaps a quick and violent reprisal. Enekorogha, where our mission station is situated, historically is a violent community, explosive and where grudges and grievances can be generational. A few years previously we had taken our clinic boat for an outreach at a small community, euphemistically called 'Elohim City'. We had informed them several days earlier that we would be coming, but on arrival the community was silent and the community hall empty of patients except one psychotic man chained to a pillar. With no psychiatric help or medication in these isolated communities, physical restraint was the only option. It prevented assault and kept the patient from absconding into the jungle or drowning in the rivers. We sought a community council member and asked what was happening. Apparently there had been a theft across a small farm boundary and an unarmed gang had left a few hours earlier in search of the miscreants responsible for the theft. It may be seen as harsh to deliver summary justice so swiftly and brutally, but in this region where there is no reliable judicial process, fines and heavy-handed punishments maintain, for the majority, a jittery status quo. Where pirate gangs are involved, summary justice is even more brutal. One gang controlling the main region around a community called Ogriagbene had tracked down a smaller rival gang muscling in on their territory, forcing them to dig their own graves beside the river before shooting them – a warning to others!

As the Pastor took one of the decrepit canoes and paddled off to wash, we considered the likelihood of an armed gang coming from Enekorogha to affect our release. After twelve days and the army unable to find us, it seemed unlikely.

The stillness of the afternoon and the soporific heat was interrupted by the sound of the speedboat. When all around is silent, oppressive and still, any new sound or movement seems exaggerated. The boatman, West, threw oil workers' overalls onto the platform.

He had an innocent face, kept himself to himself, drank a little, seemed to take no drugs, and that night, when he delivered the General to the pontoon, would rig up a mosquito net and try and sleep at the earliest opportunity. This seemed in total contrast to the others, and even before dawn he was awake and attending to the outboard on the boat. Despite his methodical approach and quiet demeanour, he had a malevolence and pent-up fury that bubbled beneath his passive exterior. One afternoon I had stood up to try and ease a stiff back but within minutes, glaring at me, he rose, picking up a machete and tapping his thigh with the blade he advanced towards me. The message was clear. I raised my hands in submission and sat down, turning away lest I incensed him more.

Anytime West was present, he exuded violence and intimidation. I was concerned to see that he had arrived on the boat alone and he was pointing at Shirley, Alanna and myself and talking to the Pastor. He had an equal disdain for the Pastor but whatever had been decided, thankfully included him.

'Each of you get on these sou'westers and put these over your heads.'

The Pastor and West had T-shirts, the necks of which they had tied into knots. In the heat the plastic of the overalls was sticky and uncomfortable, but clearly we were leaving the platform and this was to protect us against mosquito bites. We hadn't stood up for over twelve days for any time and we were dizzy as we stepped into the boats, sitting together on the middle plank seat.

The knotted T-shirts were pulled tightly down over our heads, covering our faces and neck as the boat moved out towards the creek. Our white skin would be visible to anyone, even the occasional helicopter passing overhead to the offshore oil platforms. West, the boatman, was skilled and efficient in his role, speeding briskly across the broad tributary, before easing back the throttle and the boat sinking down into the floodwaters. He cut the engine and the boat swayed as he stepped past us to begin punting us with a large bamboo pole deeper into the flooded jungle. We seemed to be back near the jetty where we had first arrived and where I had previously made the phone call. Chillingly though, we were now retracing the route deeper into the jungle toward the first smaller pontoon where we had left Ian and the nightmare of the first day. The Pastor was talking to West from the seat in front of us and we were allowed to remove our head coverings. The canopy of the trees closed over us and once more we were hidden from sight. The environment was in some way familiar, the layout of the trees, the spacing between them, and the type of creepers hanging from the trees, innocent-looking in themselves but each leaf capable of delivering a burning sting. It was only with the trained eye that one could differentiate this species from another, entirely innocuous one. The original platform had entirely disappeared.

The boat gently nudged against a small thatched hut, approximately ten by eight feet, it's bamboo floor a few inches above the floodwater. One of the longer sides was open, the other three shielded by a weathered tarpaulin lashed to the uprights of the hut by twine.

'Get out, get out, move, move.' West's tone was impatient and irritable. The Pastor was sitting on the bamboo struts of the floor; he pointed at a single mattress in the corner covered by a grey mosquito net.

'Please, get under the net,' he said, gesticulating with his left hand as he leaned on his right. He looked uncomfortable. Again, he sat nursing his right ankle that was swollen and clearly tender.

The air was thick with mosquitoes, and we sat together on the three-foot mattress, our legs crossed and our bare feet drawn tightly under us away from the edge of the net and any potential bites. A limp pillow lay at the head, filthy and with the faded print of some ducks. Beside the pillow lay a copy of the Good News Bible open to the book of Job chapter 1, and a smaller King James Bible lay unopened beside it. Two, one thousand naira banknotes poked out from somewhere in the New Testament, perhaps acting as bookmarks, perhaps as a private stash. Beside the bed lay a crudely made table, constructed from strips of bamboo and hardwood, nailed together. A stone pestle and mortar stood beside the table, and on top of the table a dirty plate. On the plate were small glass pipes and the burnt residue of what was likely cocaine or heroin.

Past the foot of the bed lay one or two rucksacks, small and black, the kind which students used as schoolbags. Some pallets of drinking water lay stacked, with two canisters of cooking gas and a sack of cassava.

Hanging from the thatch made from palm fronds twirled a small annulet on a piece of string, and a toothbrush was cleverly wedged between two fronds.

We sat in silence as West, glowering at us, pushed off, the boat quickly lost from sight as it moved back towards the creek between the trees. The Pastor was rifling through a carrier bag, finding Milo, a form of hot chocolate. He seemed pleased. He took a handful of garri from the sack and dipped it into the water before mixing it vigorously with his finger. It looked vile. He saw the expression on our faces and smiled.

'I'm hungry,' he said, chuckling, half drinking, half slurping the mixture.

'Why are we here?' Shirley asked. He shrugged, he had no idea, maybe we were leaving, he conjectured. How could he fling this idea out to us? It was one Alanna and Shirley had already dared to think.

I looked around. There was a sense of familiarity. I looked at Shirley and we both knew. Crossing the creek and punting through the bush, this was the hut that we had seen that first day just at the corner, visible from our platform, from where the young man had sourced the water and the Bible that Ian had requested. It was also quite clearly the hut from where the shots had been fired. The General, with his dog, had paddled his canoe past us to this hut. This was his personal bolt-hole. It was from here that he had killed Ian. I looked but could see no trace of our first pontoon. It was chilling to think we were sitting on his bed and even more strange that he should sleep with two Bibles and that he was currently reading the book of Job. It was as though we were revisiting the trauma of the first day, and uniquely seeing events from the assailant's perspective; but the pontoon he fired toward had gone, and so had Ian.

The Pastor lent back against the upright, obviously satiated and possibly relieved to have a change of scenery and that something at last may be happening.

An hour or two passed and nothing happened. It was uncomfortable and hot on the single mattress, unable to move, and we were sweating in the plastic overalls. The Pastor leant over, passing us a bottle of water. Alanna paused and then, in a quiet but serious tone, asked the Pastor how he had ended up in the gang. Given the quietness, and that there were no guns or drugs present and in a sense we were all marooned together, it seemed a reasonable and timely question.

The Pastor looked a little surprised and then gathered his thoughts. He seemed to appreciate the interest in himself. He whistled through his teeth. I put the Good News Bible down that I was thumbing through and we listened.

'Life you know is not easy, I was in prison eleven years, eleven years I tell you, yes-o. I was released last March, the twenty-third. I had to appeal, it took me five years and all the money I had. The barrister had to present evidence that I was not involved in a robbery but even so I spent eleven years in prison for something I did not do.' His eyes widened and paused, leaning forward to rub his ankle.

'Life in prison, you know, is not easy: there is no medication, no food unless you buy it. Your family must feed you, and, if your family don't come, then you have nothing to eat. I had to share my cell with six other people, and you have to find a way to make it work every day. I lay on my bed and would look through this very small window, like this.' He made a small square with his hands a few inches across.

'All I could see was the sky and the sun would pass over the window. I still watched the sun and kept my eyes open as long as possible until my eyes ran with tears but I wanted to see the sun so badly. I could feel the heat and the light on my eyes and I would keep looking, looking at the sun until it passed over the little window. Then, when I shut my eyes, I would see the sun for many hours after so I knew that I had seen the outside, I had seen the sun. Twenty-three hours a day I had to spend in that cell. It was there that I read the Bible. I read, I read, I read it, every day I read the word of God; that is why I know the Word of God so well.

'When I was released I went to my family that they should help me buy a small Moto so that I could be a taxi driver. Just a small job that would keep me. Why? Because I wanted a wife, but no job no wife, no house no wife, so I need a car to learn taxi. But they all turn away, my sister not help me, my brother not help me, nobody help me. So I thought to myself, okay, if there is no car then I will have to hustle. So I make my living, maybe two thousand naira a day hustling, no problem. Maybe buy mobile phone, sell for more, a little here and little there, you know I get by.

'You know I used to have a good job, I used to drive boats for oil company taking the foreign workers from shore to oil platform. In 1998 I earn ten thousand naira a month, every month, every month. But I look at the white worker. I watch him. His phone has poor signal or is slow, so he throws it into the sea, he shouts and then just buys another. When I come to platform, I see the white man lying in the sun getting colour. That's why I thought you like the sun.[1]

'I thought, why do I take the white men to the platform for ten thousand a month. There is no more opportunity. I just do the same. Seriously, I am not happy. I look at the white man and I want what he has, and that is how I left my job, to hustle and make money.'

He put down the cup he was nursing and with a wry laugh declared, 'Ten thousand naira. Look at me now; I cannot walk with this ankle, I am sitting here with you people. Just give me two thousand naira a day and I will be okay.'

The irony of giving up a well-paid job for a life of crime and eleven years in prison and now as trapped as we, in the flooded jungle of the Delta, living on scavenged food in a makeshift hut, his plans of betterment had come to nothing.

The vitriol that he expressed to his family was visceral. He declared intent to kill and maim, and then in the next breath cited his dependence on God to carry him through, to provide justice and provision. It was a self-taught theology, a creed that drew on the retribution of the God of the Old Testament. His God was one of reprisal and vindication, where justice was 'do as you would be done by'. There seemed no acknowledgement

---

1. The value of the naira has decreased dramatically over the recent decade. In 2000 the rate was almost 100 naira to the dollar, in 2018 it stands at 365. From $100 pcm in 2000 and with job security, the Pastor would, twenty years later, accept $160 pcm with no certainties.

of bad choices and living the consequences of one's own actions. It was a sad story and though the life lessons were clear, there seemed no remorse or self-examination. The paradox of sharing a little Bible study between hostages and those colluding with their kidnapper seemed lost on him. And yet for us it was a blessed opportunity to listen and to encourage him to come to Christ, to seek His will for his life, and to seek to do things God's way, when clearly his own choices had been so disastrous. There was a pathos about the man, and being able to listen and share his story, to gently prompt him to consider Christ's sacrifice and love, was valuable. He little considered the New Testament, and, though he knew many stories of Old Testament characters, the one character he seems to know least of was the person of Jesus Christ and the love that He had for him.

Our conversation was naturally drawing to an end as the sound of a distant outboard engine caused our hearts to race. Could this be our release? Was this in fact the army?

'Quick, put the Bible back as you found it,' the Pastor said. There was clear anxiety in his voice.

The familiar white and green speedboat came into view, and in the front of the boat sat a large, portly man, shaven-headed and well dressed. Behind him sat the General, by contrast looking like a waif, dressed in singlet and filthy jeans, diminutive behind the man and almost dwarfed by his automatic weapon. The contrast of body habitus and dress couldn't have been more marked.

The boat drew alongside, and the Pastor indicated we should get out and stand up. The man climbed from the boat onto the rickety poles of the platform. He stood in well-polished Cuban-heeled cowboy boots, black trousers and silver-buckled belt. He had a tight-fitting, shiny Polo shirt tucked into his trousers. He mopped his brow with a handkerchief and in the other hand held an almost industrial-sized mobile phone. He smiled, his teeth white and his skin soft and well-conditioned.

He was a man of obvious means. His boots indicated he had come from an urban area. In the creeks flip-flops, otherwise known as slippers, were really the only shoes seen, so this man had travelled some distance.

'Aah, Dr Donovan, I am the man you spoke to the other evening.' He introduced himself, but his name did not stick. He turned to Shirley, reminding himself who she was and then took Alanna's hand, repeating as much to himself her name, 'Alanna Carson'.

He apologized for the whole situation, explaining that he was an intermediary trusted by both militants and government alike. He explained that he understood the tortuous oil politics better than most, in some tacit way suggesting his involvement was with a gang of better pedigree then these 'local boys'.

After spending some time in jail, he had turned from poacher to gamekeeper and was able to penetrate any gang, given he knew he would never betray either party. He reiterated this last sentence for any shadow of doubt that may be lingering in the General's mind, given that he was standing behind him with his gun at forty-five degrees. The General, however, seemed pleased with the exchange so far, and for the one and only time he directly communicated with me, raised his left hand and gave me a slow 'thumbs-up'.

The intermediary asked if we were well, if we had had food, if we had been harmed. Questions were innocent enough, but the General, West and the Pastor scrutinized us for our responses. He asked nothing of Ian, and to have volunteered anything would have been foolish. Though this man clearly had currency with both government and the General, he himself was nevertheless vulnerable in this situation. There was no script.

He asked us if he could film us, that maybe we had a message for our families. We stood like stooges in our ridiculous outfits, sending platitudinous greetings, stilted and without expression.

The man beamed, moving the phone from each of us, then stepped back to take a general shot of the three of us. Bizarrely – and perhaps to break the obvious tension – he then declared that next time we came to Nigeria we would all go out for dinner and that he would like a photo with himself and us together. The Pastor duly obliged, and this photo would within days be in the hands of every news agency worldwide, though with our smiling Nigerian friend carefully cropped from the picture.

'We'll have you out in a couple of days,' he said, again beaming.

Shirley stepped forward, 'A couple of days you say?'

'Yes,' he said, 'a couple of days.' His voice was a little more sombre this time. He turned and beckoned for the boat. The light was beginning to go, and clearly he wanted to get back to the air-conditioned vehicle we were sure he came in. By now he too was lashed in sweat, both from the humidity and, as likely, the stress.

As he sat on the boat he turned to address the General, 'And what of the other white man?'

'We will talk ...' was all we heard the General reply, before the engine roared into life. This time West had the engine in reverse, and the surge from the wake shook the little hut.

Once more silence descended, and mosquitoes began to gather over the water. The odd 'plop' and ripple from a rising fish was the only punctuation as we withdrew once again under the mosquito net to consider the almost ludicrous exchange, and that we would not be going home today. The Pastor sat looking at the water. He had the capacity for silent inactivity, honed from years of imprisonment. He expressed no visible signs of frustration, just a passive acceptance that whatever was going to happen was going to be outside his own control. We had seen this often in Africa, where poverty and lack of resources in the face of overwhelming systemic adversity had sapped men of any initiative and of all self-belief that they could affect any change in their destiny. One time, when we had a cataract camp and numbers of patients that were far in excess of our ability to treat, Gloria, the consultant eye surgeon, looked at me and then shrugged her shoulders, 'You can only do what you can do,' she said. For many in this land, choices to do anything beyond resigned acceptance of the situation are merely dreams.

It was late afternoon when the boat returned, this time with West and another youth with a gun. By now we were quite relieved to get off the platform. In silence and with the T-shirts again over our heads, we were ferried back across the creek through the winding tributary that led to the main camp, which was now a cacophony of excitable voices, recharged by another arrival of palm wine, cocaine and marijuana.

The sense of anti-climax hung heavy.

The shrill rap music and beer-room bravado was in full swing, and from the younger men there seemed little interest in learning what had transpired. They were men of the moment, living for today, sensual and with no thought for tomorrow.

'Hey, pretty lady, aha, aha.' With his arms outstretched and limp wrists, Pharaoh swayed and sashayed toward Alanna, as she extricated herself from the heavy PVC jacket.

'That's enough,' Shirley said, with a motherly authority that Pharaoh seemed to acknowledge. He dropped his arms, smiled, then roared with laughter, a laugh that was husky and thick, beyond his twenty-seven years, coarsened by the cheap tobacco and marijuana he smoked from dawn till dusk.

Pharaoh's colleague, the more menacing of the two there, who had been so intimidating after Ian's murder, lay smiling, looking up at us. Beside him an empty bottle of peanuts and two large empty bottles of drinking water. Whilst we had been away, they had eaten and drunk almost all of our meagre provisions. High on marijuana and tramadol, it was pointless saying anything. Perhaps the initial surprise at seeing us clambering from the boat suggested that they like us were hopeful that this afternoon was to be our release. Not so.

No-name had picked up on events. As if for confirmation, he leant over when the others were distracted.

'You saw the "asset" this afternoon?' he said, looking straight at me with intent.

The term 'asset' for the intermediary was interesting; indeed he was exactly so, an asset for all parties to bring resolution to the impasse of our captivity.

It was dark and we tucked the mosquito net under the damp edges of the mattress. The empty water bottles were then pushed between the net and the mattress edge to buy those all-important inches away from the skin and any potential insect bite. We were charged with a mixture of hope and despair. There seemed something of a narrative, having seen the man behind the voice, and yet his assurance that we would be out in a day or two seemed unconvincing. Besides, how could one trust a man drawn from a militant gang to ensure safe passage of a large ransom of cash.

'You want Indomie now?' the Pastor asked. He usually cooked our single bowl of noodles around 3 p.m. each day, but today had been different. A rubber bowl of instant noodles was our only daily meal. In the first few days we may have expected some onion or a Maggi stock cube but, given that these were fortuitous items found in stolen rucksacks, we were now back to the staple dish of plain noodles. Indomie is Asian, the name drawn from Indonesia and 'mie', Indonesian for noodle. There is a vast production plant in Nigeria, and access to the product in the remotest creeks of the Delta is testimony to the efficiency of logistics and product placement. Bland yet predictable, they were a clean and reliable food source for us and we were grateful. The Pastor tried to use groundwater, but we persuaded him to use our drinking water for cooking. The evening was usually given over to exhaustive butchery and cooking of monitor lizard, and he was always keen to use the fire and get our feeding out of the way before the General arrived after nightfall. This suited us well.

He lent around the tarpaulin, handing the blackened rubber bowl to us with two forks stuck into the steaming noodles. After the following week, all of the forks would be lost into the flood and we would be down to our fingers. We said Grace, asking the Lord to bless the hands that made the food. There was a particular urgency as the Pastor had announced he was suffering from a bloody dysentery. Never washing his hands and with the bowl barely washed between meals, we prayed for a specific sanctification of the food. It was only by God's grace that we should never fall ill during our twenty-two days.

Once more the guttural sound of the General's boat reverberated through the bush. Like a menacing predator, it glided into the clearing beside the pontoon and came to rest alongside. West sat silently at the back, checking the fuel lines and shaking the petrol drums to check for fuel before removing the engine key on its fluorescent yellow cable and tucking it deep into the pockets of his shorts. The General sprung out clutching his rifle. By now the pontoon had been cleared and the evening meal in full swing. Wiza stepped forward and lent down, passing a bowl of blubbery meat atop a pile of eba, reconstituted garri. Without acknowledgement, the General took it. He sat cross-legged, his gun in his lap, and fell silent as he ate. The rest of the men sat at the periphery of the pontoon until he had eaten to his satiety, and then they worked together to pass out the remainder of the food. All were silent, and visibly relaxed once the General retreated to the boat to smoke a joint. The Pastor was gnawing at a lizard's claw. He turned it over in his hand and then handed it to Wiza. It was cooked on one side but raw on the other. Wiza shrugged. The fire had lost its heat on the metal sheet and he would have to make do. He muttered something and then carefully ate around the raw meat as you eat around a bruise on an apple.

Capon had moved to the boat, and he and the General were discussing in hushed tones what we took to be the afternoon events. Their exchange was quiet and impossible to interpret.

We lay silent. Alanna had turned away, her back to us. She had the capacity to sleep in any situation, equally when upset and, if all things were becoming too much she would withdraw. Shirley would leave her for a while before a gentle touch or a word to check she was okay.

'Grand' was the usual retort, almost never a complaint or discouraging word. She kept these to herself and shared them with her Lord. Her faith and fortitude were beyond her years, and somehow our thrown-together family on the mattress gave mutual support, one to another.

The meal was over and whilst some of the juniors lay sleeping, the seniors sat in a huddle, discussing in earnest what Shirley took to be the events of the day. Jockeying banter was always accompanied by laughter, loudness and movement. Tonight, the General held sway, his acolytes leaning in for every word. He was intentional, his voice quiet, his speech rapid and punctuated by a spit of copious phlegm or picking tobacco from his teeth.

In the dark everything seems to carry a greater significance and Shirley strained to decipher the machine gun speed of his pidgin English, to give a clue as to what was happening. The stakes were clearly high, and the demeanour of the men suggested they had little certainty that all was going to plan. It is not unknown for gangs to sell hostages when a ransom is not forthcoming. The words Boko Haram or Tompolo tumbled in and out of sentences as surely as adrenaline rose and fell with the implications of all that was said and indeed left unsaid.

The chattering ceased as the General called to Capon to pass the guitar case that belonged to Ian, hanging from one of the cross struts of the shack. Without the guitar within, the neck of the soft, black vinyl case sagged forlornly. It was heavy, containing two laptops taken at the time of our capture.

One contained all our personal details, photos and documents, and all the passwords were open. Banking, emails and music were all contained. The day before we were taken, there had been a violent electrical storm, powerful winds, lashing rain and sheets of lightning all around the mission station. The palms swayed like metronomes, the fronds whipping back and forth like a giant broom. We had stood at the windows, marvelling at the majesty of the creation, the power of the elements and the blessing of the building God had afforded us the ability to build. We had circuit breakers on all electrical equipment and the solar had been turned off, and mobiles too. I had, however, left my laptop on sleep. As the storm passed and the deafening sound of the rain against the zinc roof eased, I returned to edit some photos on the laptop. As I opened it the screen was dead, the motherboard shot through by a surge of static from a passing storm cloud.

Infuriating at the time, I now watched the General fumble with the keyboard with relief. He threw a glance to me and the Pastor told me to turn it on for him.

'I can't, it is finished, it is broken ... dead.' I drew a line with my forefinger against my throat to emphasize the point. The General understood. He knew the humidity made short shrift of electrical appliances in the creeks. He carried his cables and mobiles in a clean, sealed milk container for this very reason.

'This one, open, open now.' He pointed to the other laptop containing films and teaching material for the health workers. I did as asked. The comforting and familiar desktop image emerged, password-free, and with a familiarity that was all the more incongruous against this alien and surreal context.

'He wants to put his music on it from his phone,' the Pastor whispered. 'Please do this, now.'

Again, without the right cables, I tried to explain this was not possible. The General pulled the last hope from the guitar case, my external hard drive containing all the teaching films and pictures for the last decade.

'Battery?'

'No,' I said quietly, 'hard drive. Let me show you.' I plugged it in and revealed the files it contained. This was a new device to the General. He was puzzled and exasperated and muttered to the Pastor. The Pastor turned to me.

'He wants you to wipe it of everything and load his music onto it.'

'Okay, I can do that, but tell him I'm wiping off over ten years of teaching material that is specifically designed to help in the training of workers to serve his people, his family and communities. Tell him we do not take money for this, that we are only here to serve and show the love of our God to him.' I had had enough. Seeing the General paw at Ian's guitar case and rake around our personal belongings somehow really touched a raw nerve, and it was hard not to react.

The Pastor could see this and advised me quietly to co-operate. The red mist had fallen, and the utter lack of any respect had riled my carnal flesh.

'Tell him again Pastor, that yes, I can put his music on this if he is really happy to destroy all these years of gathering teaching material.'

The Pastor lifted himself in a buttock-shuffle nearer the General, and the surrounding elders and juniors leaned in to hear. There was a minute or two of talking, some hand gestures of up-turned palms suggesting pleading, and then they all fell back. The General paused and then rose and returned to the boat.

'He says you can have it back if and when you leave this place.' Something had been transacted at this point. Maybe a flicker of remorse or conviction, maybe some advocacy from the others who had touched something in him, something human, something with empathy.

This called to mind the strange exchange in the boat two weeks earlier when, positioned as his human shield, he gave Alanna some cream for the bites that covered her legs and arms.

It showed that no one was beyond redemption, that there was something, yes, possibly very deep, but something nevertheless that stood at variance with the visible brutality and malignity of this man. It would be so much easier to just simply have hatred for this man, to have a binary appraisal of the good and bad. But this is not how God sees us, and, like it as not, God put on us the demand to see this man as He sees him, a sinner, broken and in need of a Saviour. It required a grace beyond ourselves, and God was more than able to do this. As we confessed our conditional love, so He reminded us that His was unconditional. Were it not so, then both the General and ourselves had no hope to turn to.

# 10

# 'AND HOPE DOES NOT PUT US TO SHAME'

Daily we searched the scriptures, looking for God's will, enquiring after His ways and not ours. Certain scriptures stood out at specific times, flooding our souls with understanding, peace and hope. In Romans 5:1-2 we read: 'Therefore, since we have been justified by faith, we have peace with God through our Lord Jesus Christ. Through him we have also obtained access by faith into this grace in which we stand, and we rejoice in hope of the glory of God.'

We knew this hope would not disappoint us. It's a hope based and grounded on the love of God. He displayed His love to us when He sent His Son to die for us, in our place. We knew this hope to be an immovable rock, which became more and more the anchor upon which we fastened our faith. Because of the cross, we saw in clearer focus how God had translated us from enemies into sons and daughters. On the mattress, as the world faded, we fixed our eyes upon the glory which awaited us when we will see Him face to face, for in that day we will be like Him. We will know Him as fully as we are known. This is our hope.

This is not a spurious hope but a hope sure in the veracity of God that enables us to transcend our circumstances.

We have a promise that, as it is written: 'What no eye has seen, nor ear heard, nor the heart of man imagined, what God has prepared for those who love him.' (1 Cor. 2:9) This hope that we have as Christians is sure, no matter what the circumstances are we find ourselves in, what fiery trials we face, or what heartache we must endure. God is faithful to keep His promises, 'the hope of glory'.

Romans 5 continues in verses 3-4: 'Not only that, but we rejoice in our sufferings, knowing that suffering produces endurance, and endurance produces character, and character produces hope.' Why would we rejoice in tribulation? This was a question we asked of ourselves, and, as the difficult days crept past, we began to see the answer.

The trying of our faith is being used by God to bring about conformity to the image of His Son. Suffering without a reason can be hard to bear. When we understand the reason behind the suffering, that God is being glorified in it and we are being changed by it, we can withstand the testing of our faith. The tribulation serves to create patience. With endurance of the trial, the experience allows us to understand and know the depth of our Christian faith. Only under trial is the reality of Christian faith refined and made a tangible surety.

Romans 5:5 continues: 'And hope does not put us to shame, because God's love has been poured into our hearts through the Holy Spirit who has been given to us.' Even in the deepest trial the Holy Spirit enables us to rejoice. The remarkable transaction at the new birth gives us the spirit of the living God to dwell within us. If we allow Him full reign at those times, laying aside our own sense of self, we can rejoice in the midst of tribulation – rather the Holy Spirit rejoices through us.

Having got hold of our hope, the Bible exhorts us to take one step further with our hope. As we began to live out our understanding of what the scripture was teaching us on a mattress in the midst of the Delta, God clearly spoke to us through His Word. In 1 Peter 3:14 we read: 'But even if you should suffer for righteousness' sake, you will be blessed. Have no fear of them, nor be troubled.' These were words straight from the throne of grace for the situation we found ourselves in. In the face of the terror caused by our captors, we were exhorted not to be afraid nor be troubled, and indeed encouraged to be happy in suffering for righteousness' sake. No words could be more applicable to us at this time. The scripture goes on in verse 15: 'But in your hearts honor Christ the Lord as holy, always being prepared to make a defense to anyone who asks you for a reason for the hope that is in you; yet do it with gentleness and respect.' The opportunity to do this arose when at different times one or more of the men asked us how we could pray, laugh and show no anger toward them. At this point we were able to expound upon our hope and witness to the saving grace of Jesus Christ, and to share the reason for the hope we had.

They watched us and were baffled by how we became more settled over the weeks and able to express and experience joy in the situation. We had no shame in the gospel that afforded us hope, and we were emboldened to unashamedly testify of the beauty and grace of Jesus Christ.

We came to realize the hope we were holding onto was, and is, the person of Jesus Christ. Everything we have, or will ever need, is in Him.

Hope is not an abstract concept, not an emotion or feeling. There is a difference between hope as the world knows it and biblical hope. The hope spoken of in scripture is the gospel and all that it entails, here and in the world to come. The gospel is the person of Jesus Christ. As Paul writes in Colossians 1:27: 'To them God chose to make known how great among the Gentiles are the riches of the glory of this mystery, which is Christ in you, the hope of glory.' In 1 Timothy 1:1 he writes: 'Paul, an apostle of Christ Jesus by command of God our Saviour and of Christ Jesus our hope.'

'And hope does not put us to shame.' The second aspect of this scripture to be grasped is embodied in the word 'ashamed'. There was no doubt that we experienced shame in our captivity, something we railed against, being put in that position. Scantily clad, unwashed, matted hair, coated teeth and smelling, we watched our captors wash and preen themselves daily, applying cream to their skin, lotions from stolen rucksacks and fragrant soaps. Behind a greying mosquito net and covered in mite bites, there was little to raise our self-esteem. We felt ashamed in our condition and, for a lot of the time, we despised the shame – it made us feel disadvantaged before our captors, eating noodles from a single bowl with our fingers. We felt like animals.

We realized how uncomfortable it was to feel shame. In a broader way we try at all costs to avoid shame. We do not enjoy reproach, humiliation or disgrace, yet all these emotions are exactly what Jesus Christ underwent for our salvation. Shame is a painful emotion, and we caught a glimpse of the pain of Jesus Christ.

> Despising the shame: one of the prominent elements of the torture of the cross was its extreme shame. Jesus did not welcome this shame – He despised it – yet He endured through it to victory. Daniel 12:2 states that shame will be an aspect of the terrors of hell. ('And many of them that sleep in the dust of the earth shall awake, some to everlasting life, and some to shame and everlasting contempt.') Jesus bore this hellish shame to accomplish our redemption. Shame itself is a trial. Jesus bore shameful accusation, mocking, beating, a crown of thorns, a shameful robe; even as He prayed on the cross He was shamefully mocked.[1]

So why then do we as Christians find shame such a stumbling block? We seem to be able to do anything for Jesus except

---

1. David Guzik's commentary on Hebrews 12, 'The Enduring Word', www.enduringword.com/bible-commentary/

endure shame for His name. If we are to be able to identify with our Saviour we must embrace shame.

We realized there was still too much of ourselves and not enough of Jesus. If we were to please only Him and not man, then shame would not be something to run from. 'For am I now seeking the approval of man, or of God? Or am I trying to please man? If I were still trying to please man, I would not be a servant of Christ.' (Gal. 1:10)

Surely, we reasoned, this was the crux of the matter. If we live our life before Christ and Him alone then the opinions of man fade, and indeed, the embracing of shame brings us into closer communion with our Saviour.

It is also comforting to know that He will not put more upon us than we can bear. 'No temptation has overtaken you that is not common to man. God is faithful, and he will not let you be tempted beyond your ability, but with the temptation he will also provide the way of escape, that you may be able to endure it' (1 Cor. 10:13).

Our God is faithful through all trials; indeed He walks through them with us as He promised never to leave or forsake us. It is only in trial as you choose to look to Him that this truth becomes a reality. This truth was made a reality for us.

# 11

# SOMETHING'S GOT TO GIVE

It was day twenty-two. It hadn't rained for some days and the flood was receding. In three to four weeks this area would be once more land, sandy and dense in foliage. Rivulets would run from the interior of the bush to the tidal creeks and rivers drain into the Atlantic. Along these tidal runs small traps would be fixed to the mud by bamboo spikes to catch crayfish, abundant at this time. Deeper in the jungle, low lying areas would be cut off from the rivers, large pools with catfish plentiful and unable to escape, and easy to catch. This would be a time of plenty, with many people returning to their fishponds in the interior to see what the floods had left behind. New cassava crops would be planted, the alluvial soil now rich from the floodwaters and the sediments left behind. With the floods gone we would soon be discovered, and the men knew this.

Each day with the water level falling, tree stumps slowly emerged from the flood, and now there was a clear eighteen inches between the bamboo of the floor and the waters. The water was stagnant, still, with a rainbow hue of oil from cooking monitor lizards spreading over the brown water. All around the pontoon lay the detritus of water bottles, wrappers, faeces and algae blooms, a haze of insects hovering over the turbid morass, the smell pungent and strong as the sun rose.

Only the surge of the General's boat caused any disturbance to the water each evening on arriving, and again on morning departure. The men seemed oblivious to the toxic soup and risk of disease, but it was noticed they chose to paddle a little away now by canoe to wash and drink the water.

For us, however, there was no choice. We had stockpiled empty water bottles with rain that had dripped from the thatched roof, but the supply was now very low, and we could not lean to wash ourselves by the mattress as the drop to the water was too great and the risk of infection too high.

The men were tangibly irritable. Drugs were less available and food was limited. We continued to have a bowl of noodles each day but now, eating with our fingers and without the ability to wash, we nipped the noodles between finger tips, spat upon and wiped against the cleanest edge of a tee shirt. Water was in shorter supply, coming in one or two bottles at a time, and groundnuts or biscuits were scarce. The men were hungry, fed up, and tempers were frayed.

The night had been like all others, a cacophony of rap music and action movies played on numerous competing phones. Every three hours the shift on watch changed, and those returning had no intention of slipping onto the pontoon quietly. Capon and Wiza talked raucously most of the night, like teenagers trying to outdo each other in extremes of criminal behaviour. By the first hint of dawn they were fading and would become resentful of morning activities as they tried to sleep.

The drums of the distant fetish temples began their slow thumping, and the Pastor sat up to call the crew to the bizarre ritual of morning devotions to seek divine sanction and protection for all the efforts of the General and the obliteration of his enemies. We had never joined with the Pastor to sing choruses, a point not missed by some of the men, puzzled that as Christians we did not enthusiastically join in the devotions. The Pastor had not pushed the point, and we believed this to be in some sense conviction.

This morning was heavy, and each of us awoke with a pervading sense of despair. It would be wrong to have shared this but we each had a sense that things were drawing to a close one way or another. This had all gone on far longer than anyone could have imagined. Both Alanna and Shirley believed this day was significant, and I too had concerns that time was running out. With no sense that the money was forthcoming and faltering communiques from the intermediary, we had the sinking feeling that the General may decide to simply cut his losses, given the receding protection of the floods.

It was against this that Shirley kneeled to squat against the edge of the mattress. I loosely held her wrap in front of her to waist height to add a modicum of decency, given fourteen men also shared the little pontoon each night. I looked out across the water and knew that illness was inevitable unless we got out soon. The situation was untenable.

Pharaoh was loud and irritable, the youth with the filthy shorts was shouting at So'ja, and, to one side, West slowly donned his now greying vest before stepping nimbly onto the speedboat beside the pontoon, without comment or acknowledgement of the others. Almost silent amidst the men, he snored heavily all night. It was a curious paradox.

The General sat cross-legged. Around him fussed two of the men, flicking water over him and offering him some cold lizard and eba. He ate without comment. The protective rituals done, he rose and, catlike, stepped into the boat, clutching – as he did in his sleep – his AK-47.

The engine surged and rose on the water, a plume of blue smoke enveloping West at the stern and, standing, he lowered the throbbing propeller shaft into the turbid water. The propeller churned the murky water and he guided the boat into the small tributary leading to the main creek, the

General seated, silent, flanked by two of the elders. As always with his departure, the atmosphere on the pontoon eased a little.

At night there were seventeen of us crammed onto the pontoon like sardines, fourteen of the men and the three of us. Besides the phone call and meeting the 'asset', we had never left the mosquito net the whole twenty-one days on this pontoon, but each night two others were erected for the seniors, and the General had one for himself (and his rifle). Wedged between the nets, the younger men tried their best to fend off the mosquitoes, restless and irritable with their constant whine and bites. It was small wonder that by now almost all the men were suffering malaria, some just irritable and achy, others febrile and ever desirous of sleep.

Drugs ameliorated the pain and brought a fitful sleep.

In the dawn, the opiate haze was dissipating, and withdrawal was waking many. Those who had sat for hours at watch were heavy with sleep. Mobile phones shrilled with tinny rap music and expletive-laden vocals. When the battery died, one of the men silently glided away on a canoe, only to return some hours later with the phones recharged and sometimes with a few packets of marijuana. There must be access to a generator not too far away, though far enough distant that we never heard the two-stroke din. It was clear that a community lay maybe a mile or two away, complicit and abetting.

With the General gone the men started to wake, irritable and raucous. I continued to fix my eyes on the waters in front of me; it would be unwise to lock gaze with anyone at this point.

Then, the silence fell. Around the pontoon the birds seemed to quieten, the mobile phones became silent and the men became still, and all activity ceased. The atmosphere changed and from somewhere and nowhere, the sound of a piano was heard, the keys loud, with a slight echo at the end of each note, bass, and the sound full. The line of music repeated itself and then ... a voice ... white, male, American most likely, and with a backing orchestra, full and ambient, as the music filled the surroundings around our miserable pontoon, full and with depth as if coming from a vast and costly sound system,

> God will make a way, where there seems to be no way,
> He works in ways we cannot see,
> He will make a way for me,
> He will be my guide, hold me closely to His side,
> With love and strength for each new day,
> He will make a way, He will make a way.
>
> By a roadway in the wilderness He leads me,
> Rivers in the desert will I see.
> Heaven and earth will fade, but His word will still remain,
> And He will do something new, today ...[1]

The verses repeated twice over and faded. The music gently died and, almost as the last note faded, the cacophony and brittle music from the phones resurged. The men unfroze and went about their business, and what we should term normality in this situation returned.

The music was gone. The madness had resumed. I looked at Shirley.

'Did you hear that?' she said, redressing as best as she could. 'That was unbelievable.'

Alanna was sitting up, unable to speak. There were no words to describe the impact this song had, its timeliness, context, its message and effect. There was no doubt to any of us, God had spoken into this situation and had done so sovereignly. We had until now never heard a western voice or English lyrics, and never with such a full-bodied sound. The

---

1. From the song *God Will Make a Way* by Don Moen, 1987.

song had laid itself over the pontoon like a sweet-smelling aroma, filling the pontoon with the tangible presence of God and an anointing we had never before experienced. We had real peace, joy and a sense of expectation we hadn't dared to hope for. Could it be that our God was going to do something new – today? Was it such that He had spoken and was He going to intervene in time and our temporal existence, to effect change for His glory? We prayed this to be the case.

The men around us seemed oblivious and had settled into their daily routine of smoking, banter and, in turns, paddling out to cleaner water to wash and toilet. So'ja aggressively thrashed at a bamboo stem with a machete to cut a length for the fire that Wiza was starting, He blew, and sparks and smoke engulfed his head. He recoiled, spluttering and cursing. The flames danced and died.

He stepped back and, taking a tin, sprinkled some kerosene on the smouldering mess. There was a loud thump and the whole mass ignited. So'ja poked and removed the more incendiary pieces of foliage. He laughed, delighting in the chaos and madness of it all.

Alanna, Shirley and I sat silently, watching the proceedings around us. Today was significant; we each believed that God had spoken. Beside us, No-name, whom we now called Abe, sidled up, shifting from buttock to buttock, until he could whisper. He beamed.

'You know,' he looked anxiously around him before continuing, 'last night I dreamt that this night, yes tonight, I will be sleeping in my own bed.' He too had perceived that today held significance. He slunk back, leaning against an upright, and his gaze went to the distance.

From far away another loud thump and crash, other more shadowy members of the gang were testing explosives somewhere in another creek.

The sun had risen and so had the heat. Pharaoh had left early carrying a machete. He returned dusty and wet with sweat. We had heard the sound of wood being cut and branches falling into the water for some time. He smiled. He was clearly happiest when doing something; he was strong, virile and unable to be still unless, like a young spaniel, he was utterly exhausted.

He called to Capon and the youth with the filthy shorts. He lowered himself into the flood some metres from the pontoon, feeling with his feet for something lying on the jungle floor. He rose, taking a deep lung full of air, and dived. He came up slowly, pulling to the surface the end of a large, thick trunk of a felled palm tree. Capon did likewise to catch the other end.

Some four metres in length, they called to So'ja to bring one of the hidden speed boats some yards away, half hidden in the creepers and palm fronds. The trunk was lifted across the boat and, in minutes, another three tree trunks had been lifted from the floodwaters and tied together across the boat. Pharaoh pulled himself onto the stern, careful not to displace the boat and lose the timber. He stood and, with a bamboo pole, started to punt the craft deeper into the trees where he had been so active earlier.

It was a cunning idea. A prefab pontoon structure, ready-made and secreted in the floodwaters that can be moved and a new base erected in just a matter of hours. It was unsurprising that the gang had not been caught, with many of these structures dotted around the creeks and identical to any other village hut. The gang was large, some forty-five men, yet made up of small units dotted in remote and carefully concealed localities. They could move between a vast number of these shacks, almost viral in spread, with no real central base, and never all together at the same time.

As we sat, slightly discouraged by the ingenuity of the gang, Abe once more approached us, this time with more ease as the others were now few, most distracted with this extra activity and diversion.

'We must have a Bible study today. But first, tell me why you always read the New Testament? I love to read the Old Testament, I love the stories.'

Shirley explained the fulfillment of the Old Covenant in the New, how Jesus came to fulfil the Law of which the Prophets wrote. Abe was silent. This was obviously new to him.

Fetish belief and idol worship was one directional, and any perceived blessing from a pagan deity came from a prescribed ritual-based service. The concept of a loving God, who desires a relationship with His creation such that He would facilitate this through the very sacrifice of His own son, was a total anathema. A love-based theology was beyond comprehension. Sacrifice under the Old Covenant made more sense. The person of Jesus was a paradox and it was so sad to see. For the preceding weeks we had taken every opportunity to share who Christ is and convey His love to this young man.

Once more he drew back. He smiled, to disarm us.

'Today, you lady, will discuss the book of Zechariah.' He pointed at Shirley and then, more seriously, he turned to me. We had started tentatively the preceding day, and Abe had heard our efforts.

'You, Mr David, I give you maybe 50 per cent but your lady I give 90 per cent, so she should explain the book.'

I felt admonished, but he was right. Shirley had a particular ability to communicate and a better understanding of Old Testament prophetic writing. She was hesitant, knowing this was a difficult book, and prayed once again with earnestness that the Holy Spirit would equip us and give revelation.

'But you will explain chapter 12, Mr David. Why? Because it is bitter. Then your lady will explain chapter 13, because once more it is sweet.' Abe was smart and his humour was razor sharp, but caustic to be on the end of. I smiled a smile of insincerity.

And so the late morning turned to afternoon and we concluded the study, breaking only for some bread and a little water. Abe had read this book often, and his questions were well prepared and intelligent.

At the outset of the study the Pastor, sensing a chance, had eased himself over to us and tried, clumsily, to take control of the little group. He had little understanding of the gospel and even less desire to apply it to his own life. It was a curious paradox and soon he gave up. Abe's natural intelligence ran rings around him and, not being able to dominate, he had little interest in listening.

Abe leant on an elbow and thanked Shirley for her exposition. He looked satisfied with what he had heard and turned over to lie on his back to digest all he had had explained to him.

Alanna interjected before he could fully relax.

'Can I ask you a question?'

'Of course,' he said smiling.

'How will it benefit you if you gain the whole world from this and then lose your soul? What's your answer to this?' It was a question he was not prepared for. He paused.

'Let me answer that one tomorrow' he replied with an apologetic smile. 'By all that you have been saying, I am, at present, let me say 51 per cent persuaded.'

He rolled over, pointing his finger once more, 'Tomorrow we will do Timothy.'

'The book about the men stealers?' I replied. The irony was not lost on him. He smiled and turned away.

Pharaoh had returned, sweat-soaked and in high spirits, his pent-up energies drained by frenetic cutting and chopping. He stripped his vest off and took a canoe a little way off to wash in the marginally cleaner water rather than the stagnant soup around the shack.

Returning, he had the air of someone satisfied with a day's work and clearly relieved to have had some time away from the claustrophobia of the little platform we shared. He leant down and shook Wiza from his drug-soaked dreams behind the tarpaulin.

'Give me smoke now, come on.' Wiza, barely conscious, flapped his arms. There were no cigarettes, only the tail end of marijuana, which Pharaoh seized with alacrity. Wiza cursed and, too tired in the afternoon heat, he turned over on his front and, with his head on his hand, he almost immediately fell into reverie.

Pharaoh reached for a small polythene bag wedged between the fronds of the roof. He took a handful and chewed on them, leaning over the pontoon to take a cupped hand of the brown brackish water to swallow them down. He lay on his back, pulled his white vest up to expose and cool his abdomen, and fell asleep. He barely moved for three hours, the sun beating down on him, small beads of perspiration swelling on his brow before running in rivulets down his face and neck. He had taken tramadol, a synthetic opiate, a drug of endemic abuse among the young of Nigeria. He had taken 3,000 mg with marijuana. The maximum dose prescribed is 400 mg, yet it only sedated him for a couple of hours. He awoke as So'ja, who seemed hopelessly intoxicated and incendiary with the mildest of stimulants, fell onto him, pushed in annoyance by Wiza. The afternoons were times when most slept, the sun and the heat at their zenith.

Pharaoh heaved So'ja off him and pulled himself upright. A dog only needs a sleep cycle of ninety minutes to be refreshed and Pharaoh seemed to need little more. He saw we were awake and shuffled between Abe and me, stretching himself out.

Shirley whispered to me to speak to him, to tell him of Jesus once more. Pharaoh was the same age as our younger son and, despite his volatility, there was still a childish side. He liked to talk. Over the three weeks, a fragile rapport had been made, surprisingly given he was the most violent and unpredictable toward us at the start. There was enough credit to ask a question with some risk.

'How did you come to be involved in all this?' I asked him, pausing to see if this was going to cross any unwritten line. It didn't. He rubbed his eyes from the smoke. The marijuana had relaxed him.

'I was at school but my mother, she couldn't manage, so I had to leave.' To 'manage' in this context meant pay the fees, really only a stipend, but so often a deal-breaker for so many living on subsistence farming and fishing.

'I drifted, I have nothing, so I had to do something, and this now is my family. The General, he taught me many things, guns, building. He taught me everything so now I move with him.' He shrugged.

'And your father?'

He became animated 'I saw him this year, for the first time, since was young. I went to see him.'

He beamed, it was obviously an important day. The smile was transitory.

'I have not seen him again, he has thirty-five children, yes now, seriously, thirty-five I am telling you.' He said this almost boasting, and yet it only highlighted his own isolation, a father only in name.

'But you have a heavenly father, who loves you more than your own father could ever love you.' The words held him silent and he listened expressionless. It was as if the words were being sown directly into his spirit; without distraction or noise he was giving me his whole attention. For the first time I laid out the redemptive plan of salvation and he listened. No interruption, no point-scoring caustic aside from the Pastor, no order, nothing. Shirley reinforced everything with constant reference to our own sons. The familial, paternal aspect of God's love was not lost on Pharaoh.

After a time there seemed a natural pause, a conclusion of matters. I had nothing left to say. We turned to each other. As one, we felt that we had said all that could be said. The gospel had been delivered, fully and from several angles. It was as if the work was complete, and the urgency to press in more was satiated.

Even Pharaoh looked at peace.

'You know me as Pharaoh, but in my village I have another name, "Story King". I can tell many stories, I will tell you one.'

And so this volatile, murderous, drug-fuelled youth transitioned into another person altogether, gentle, laughing at his own stories, childish shaggy-dog stories about Mr and Mrs Goat and their delicate relationship with neighbours, Mr and Mrs Lion. The stories were simple, inane and harmless, the sort you would tell a young child before bed. It was as if the fragment of this youth was speaking, an aspect of his arrested development, that had not fully integrated with the sensual, danger-seeking sibling that was his older, uncharted self.

By now the sun had started to lower in the sky behind our heads, though its heat was still high, and, encouragingly, the shadows were starting to lengthen. The Pastor was awake and reached his hand out for a water bottle.

'Indomie?'

'Thank you.' We untucked a corner of the mosquito net and passed out a bottle two-thirds full. It only left one half bottle for drinking, and the box of Indomie was now almost empty, with maybe one or two left. No more provisions had arrived, and it was disconcerting to see how little water was now left.

After some minutes, the familiar black rubber bowl was passed under the net, full of twisted ribbons of anaemic-looking instant noodles. We prayed for the sanctification of the food and for a blessing on the hands that made it. With no forks, we spat on our fingers and rubbed them against a trace of toilet paper. Dysentery was now almost inevitable, especially given the Pastor was ill with it and we would soon have to face local food cooked with river water.

The noodles were fuel, nothing more, and we ate them with intention, just grateful for this provision.

As we finished, the familiar growl of a 75 horsepower outboard could be heard out on the creek. It was too early for the General so perhaps a local vigilante group?

The fire on the metal sheet was extinguished and everyone was still, Capon loading the pump action shotgun and taking up a position facing the narrow entrance to the clearing.

The engine noise grew louder and then the familiar cry of 'Owwoo!'

Capon lowered his gun. The General's boat swept into the small clearing, the General sitting in the front with all the 'elders' behind him, clutching automatics and solemn of expression.

The engine cut, and West jumped to tie the boat, the youth with the filthy shorts kneeling to pull the boat against the pontoon so the elders could disembark.

Silently and without acknowledgement they each stepped from the boat, leaving the General in the front of the boat rolling a joint, his gun laid across his lap and his small dog at his feet. It was clear the dog was not a pet, but for watch when he slept. Nevertheless, it had a benign expression and a constant whine of worry.

Nothing was said for some minutes. We sat up, concerned at this new development and had prayed as soon as the engine was heard, again relinquishing our worries to the Lord. It was a strange fact that even with the constant threat of danger, there was a real comfort in routine, and any new development brought into sharp focus the precariousness of our situation.

When the General had finished his joint, he beckoned the Pastor. His ankle swollen and painful, the Pastor used his powerful shoulders to shuffle himself across to the boat. There followed some minutes of hushed talking, then the Pastor turned to us.

'The Master wants to know what you will say to anyone about your number two.' By this he meant Ian.

'I would first say he was never my number two but my equal and brother in Christ. I will say whatever the General would wish me to say on this matter.' This was not a time to negotiate. There was clearly movement happening in respect to our capture, but in what way it was impossible to say. I felt, for the first time since hearing the song earlier in the day, a sense of expectancy.

The General nodded. He clearly understood me but chose to use the Pastor as his intermediary.

Again they conversed.

'The Master says you should say he died of not eating.'

It would seem to anyone that this was an absurdity.

'I will tell them this,' I replied.

'The Master also wants you to tell the authorities that the people they have arrested so far in connection with your taking have nothing to do with the situation. You need to tell them and get them released.'

'I will do so certainly; if I do not recognize them, then I will say so.' This gave the very real hope that we would be speaking to authorities, but in what manner? Would it be on another pontoon with another intermediary coming to film us? It seemed the most likely scenario, and one the General could observe. He could see if we lied and take the appropriate steps once we were back on the pontoon.

Again he fell silent and this time cocaine pipes came out and cigarettes for the others. No one spoke.

The sun was still above the trees, but only just, and the first shadows were now touching our heads; it must be around five in the late afternoon.

Again, after a little while, the elders retired back to the boat. The men on the pontoon, Capon, Wiza, Pharaoh, Abe, Pastor, So'ja and the youth with the filthy shorts sat silent, clearly without any idea what was 'on the ground' as local people would say in such a situation.

We waited.

In the Delta few can affect change quickly. Rains, floods, heat and the difficulty of communication, the environment and transportation mean that often all one can do in a situation is to wait for whatever the hindrance is to pass. This time it was the light of day.

Here, in the midst of the jungle, somewhere in the Niger Delta seventeen people sat in silence. They sat for over two hours and barely a word was spoken. In each head there must have been a conversation and each one so different. Alanna thinking of her home in Ireland, Irish stew at the farmhouse table, her calling to mission and surrender to God's path at such a young age; Shirley and I thinking of our sons and all God had taken us through; Abe thinking of Belarus and a new life, Capon his girlfriend at Patani; Pastor, a new car and life as a taxi driver; and for each other member, a new life bankrolled by whatever largesse was to be given by the General for their part. For some, however, this was their life. It was not actually all about money for changed circumstances. They were outlaws and nomadic. Bravado, drugs and autonomy were all they sought. Yet these were the most entrapped – in bondage to sensual experience, addiction, adrenaline and cruel task masters – and with no capacity for escape, for they could never escape themselves and all that internally drove them.

At the moment when the penumbra of twilight became night, in unison the elders arose and regathered on the pontoon. West and Capon punted to the trees a little way off and withdrew the concealing foliage from a second boat. They took a boat each and silently punted to the pontoon.

'Come.' The Pastor beckoned us from the mosquito net.

The life jacket I used as a pillow was pulled and thrust into my hands.

'Put it on. You two,' pointing at Shirley and Alanna. 'Put life jacket on.'

We did as told and stood there, Shirley was last to stand. I looked down. She was folding our precious Bible in two, and then with both hands, tried to push it into the side pocket on my cargo pants. I helped as I stepped toward the boat, the Pastor indicating we should embark.

Abe stood silent against the upright, expressionless. I looked at him as I passed. I lay a hand on his shoulder and, looking at him, whispered, 'Get out of this madness.'

The Pastor brusquely brushed my hand away.

'No time for that, enter the boat, now, now.'

I sat on the wooden bench as Shirley and Alanna were assisted into the boat. Our legs were weak and we were dizzy standing, having lain for so long. The boat was the same as the one that took us. An A23 with five bench seats, each accommodating three people. Behind us sat the General. He tapped me on the shoulder. I turned. He looked at me and, from his cargo pants he withdrew the hard drive and handed it to me. Shirley looked at him as she stepped in and said, 'Thank you, General.' He looked surprised and awkward, finding it difficult to look Shirley in the eyes.

We sat down. Pharaoh turned to us. He was sitting on the bench in front, on the right side. He handed three African wraps.

'Cover your heads with these and bend down, seriously.'

We did as asked, the rigid foam of the life jacket pressing into our throats making it hard to breathe.

I caught a glimpse of all the elders in the boat alongside us. There was a slight lilt to ours and I perceived the General quickly changing boats.

Behind us West was trying to start the engine. The electronic start was broken, and he coiled and recoiled the pull cord, pulling with a grunt each time. The engine spluttered, trying to catch before falling silent. Again and again he tried until, finally, the petrol cleared and the engine caught. A heavy 'clunk' and the gears engaged and we moved forward, the exhaust popping and spluttering and the acrid engine smoke engulfing us.

We each crouched, with no idea where we were going and why. The portent from the early morning that something was to happen today was indeed coming true, but for better, or worse? Was this the terminating event of a failed kidnap or the move to release. Our thoughts swung from hope to despair. Had we been sold to a rival gang or, worse still, Boko Haram – it had been mooted before? I had assumed we would retrace our path back to the creek but, instead, the engine barely turned over, and all around us frogs and toads called for mates and the nocturnal fauna of the Delta jungle began to stir. Cries of bats, a despairing coarse cry permeated the darkness and some pops and trills of unknown birds.

'Mr David, keep down.' A heavy hand pushed my shoulder down as a branch clawed me in passing. We were clearly going deeper through the flooded jungle, weaving between trees and with no obvious torch assisting us. Small wonder the army could not find us – the land was devoid of landmarks and known only to the indigenes born and raised in this land.

All were silent on the boat as we inched through the trees and vines for maybe one to two hours.

Then we stopped. To our right a faint glow of a fire and some voices indicated we were beside either another pontoon or land. The voices were low. The engine was idling.

I inched the wrap to one side and, without raising my head, could see in the fire and moonlight some water hyacinth gently bobbing beside the boat. This must be a creek, as it only grows in the rivers.

We sat still. No one spoke, and the voices nearby fell silent. After ten minutes a faint sound of an engine was audible up ahead. It whined and screamed at very obviously high revs and was coming right for us from up ahead. As it neared, the engine fell back and the revs slowed, the boat sinking down audibly and the resulting bow wave hitting our boat, causing it to rock violently.

The voice was the General's, excitable, staccato and rapid. The throttle opened and his boat accelerated away behind us. Again, there was silence and as the wake passed the boat once more settled.

Then quietly, we began to move forward. Slowly and steadily we covered maybe three hundred metres before we slowed, the boat stopping as it scraped against a mud bank. This was the first land we had seen in three weeks. There was a pause, a short exchange between two on our boat, then a commotion.

'Take your life belts off quickly, now.' The voice was stern and emphatic.

Pharaoh tore the wraps from our heads and cried, 'Go, go!'

To the left two silhouettes leaned down and out from a sloping river bank, their hands open to grasp ours.

I stepped from the boat, stumbling up the three-metre bank, my legs weak and with little co-ordination. Behind me Shirley and Alanna followed. At the top I turned, the water was boiling, the engine screaming, as the boat turned and sped away before shots could be fired.

In front as we climbed up we saw a 4x4 facing away, its doors open, lights on and all hazard lights flashing. Silhouettes of soldiers stood all around and one silhouette stood out against the glare of the lights.

Shirley walked over and embraced him. It was the intermediary, the 'asset' who had come to film us as we sat in the General's hut. He smiled and embraced her.

As we stepped from the dirt road into the leathery smelling cool interior of the 4x4 we stepped from one world into another.

The man in the driver's seat sat motionless, some soft, middle of the road R'n'B purring from the sound system.

The change from captive to free had been immediate, unexpected and complete. For just this little moment in this vehicle, there were no words to articulate what had just happened, no words to express the jumble of emotions and thoughts. We let the music play as the convoy began to move out along the road, bemused bystanders beside the occasional fire and homestead, watching this string of vehicles pass by, illuminating for a moment the dense blackness of their night.

We turned to each other, recalling the voice we had heard at dawn, this day:

'God will make a way, where there seems to be no way,
He works in ways we cannot see,
He will make a way for me ...
Heaven and earth will fade, but His word will still remain,
And He will do something new, today ...[2]

---

2. Ibid.

# 12
# STRUGGLE

*For you have died, and your life is hidden with Christ*
*in God (Col. 3:3).*

For nearly fifteen years we thought we had put everything
down and that we really believed that to live is Christ and
to die is gain (Phil. 1:21). But during this testing period we
realized we only had a mental assent to this scripture and
not a surrender to the full implications contained therein. It
had been very easy when death was a distant fact, and living
for Christ, even on the mission field, meant discomfort and
some danger, but in reality, we had been protected by Christ
in a very difficult area. We had got used to feeling sheltered
and secure. Despite one previous attempt to kidnap us, there
was still a complacency that had crept in. Perhaps we had
even taken for granted that we had protection, and that this
would never be part of God's plan for us. In the earlier days
we were much more aware of the dangers, as the experience
was still new, alien, and the dangers were very much in the
front of our minds. We had counted the cost, however, and
still believed it was a cost and a threat worth taking. Even on
the first morning following our capture, we still felt somehow

sure that we would get out quickly and unharmed. This false security lasted until our dear friend Ian was shot, at which point everything changed. Immediately we were confronted with the fact that these men would kill. This had never been considered a reality in my mind, but one that was to be with us daily.

As we read the Bible, this scripture became a challenge. It was no longer a glib assent, but we had to search our hearts; was this in fact true and how deep did this conviction go? Was Christ enough in this situation? It was very easy to proclaim this scripture in the midst of medical camps, when we were the focus of the business and in the melee of all the missionary activities. Even at home that continued. All was for God, planning and going to Nigeria, speaking, sourcing equipment, being 'busy'; it was all for Him, all for Jesus. We truly believed this. We did what the Bible told us not to do, we looked around and compared ourselves with other Christians around us. 'But when they measure themselves by one another and compare themselves with one another, they are without understanding' (2 Cor. 10:12).

We measured ourselves by other Christians and believed we were fully surrendered. We had put career choices on the altar, along with potentially high earnings and pension security. We had made what we thought were good choices about how and where we lived, cutting our cloth, foregoing previously extravagant holidays and investing our finances into the work of God. We had thrown out the television more than ten years ago, using our time wisely, being serious about our faith and rejecting increasingly the things of the world. We had gone further in aligning our lives with what we believed were God's wishes and in being serious about living out what we believed to be true.

As simply stated by Hudson Taylor, 'If God is not Lord of all, then He is not Lord at all.' Empirically, we agreed this to be true and we had set our life so. We felt perhaps rather self-satisfied about the seeming 'depth' of our walk, little knowing to what depth this was to be challenged.

Within eighteen hours of our capture we had a new understanding of the seriousness of our predicament. We were about to be tested, how deeply we truly understood the scripture, that 'for to me to live is Christ, and to die is gain'. At this point the text from Job 2:4 better described our situation: 'Skin for skin! All that a man has he will give for his life.' We had been gripped with fear and uncertainty, and our desperate prayers were that God would deliver us from this situation. As we huddled together, it was for survival that we prayed. We were ready to agree to anything to save our lives. We talked about selling everything, borrowing money from family and wherever to secure our release. We were going to work this out using all our own ingenuity and persuasive skills, and that God would come alongside us in this endeavour. God, however, had a very different plan. He began to make it clear that we were praying for the wrong things and in the wrong way. We had to stop praying for our release. Instead, we should ask for His will to be done, and that He would teach us what He had for us to learn in this situation.

We thought back to the scripture God had given us on the outward flight where we were to 'strengthen what remains'. This didn't just apply to the work - as we thought - but to us personally. We had to wrestle with that scripture, and in the reality we were now in. Everything had looked good before, and we had convinced ourselves that everything was good, but God had blown the lid off. It was actually our own lives that looked alive but had elements that were about to die. These must be strengthened. It was at this point we had a conscious choice. We could continue in self-delusion, thinking all was well, ignoring the prompting of the Holy Spirit. Or we could accept the chastening of the Lord and be open to the promise that God disciplines the one He loves (Heb. 12:5-12).

If for me to live was Christ, then everything inside had to change. How could I represent Christ with anger, resentment and bitterness in my heart? How could I claim my life was Christ when survival was uppermost in my thoughts? How could my life be Christ when all I could think about were my sons? Would I see them ever again? There was no longer the liberty to set aside this train of thought. At home I could always push aside things that were uncomfortable and deal with them at another point. Suddenly, everything demanded that full attention be put on these thoughts and battles. I was reduced to the point where the scripture 'to work out your own salvation with fear and trembling' (Phil. 2:12) had to be applied to myself.

How sure was I of what I believed? How sure was I in whom I put my trust? It was a process of deconstructing everything to look at it afresh without the luxury of deferring to a more convenient point. It had to be now. I had to wrestle with all these doubts that were assailing me before God. It was all consuming, to deal with issues now. There was no choice, there was no escape, no distraction, an intense visceral discomfort in every sense, seeing my faith deconstructed on the mattress. I was under conviction for having put off in the past these very issues.

I began to do as 2 Corinthians 13:5 exhorts us to do, to 'examine' myself. In so doing I was convinced Jesus Christ was indeed in me. Grappling with these truths in honesty before Christ, He ministered peace to my soul. At that point He showed me the need for an honest walk before Him. Sitting and fitting in with a white middle-class church culture was not adequate and was hypocritical. It was ironic. In Nigeria we toiled to awaken our workers to see beyond the African Christ they had formed through worship prayer and favoured doctrine. Yet we had done the same in our culture. I had not seen it, but we were the same. It was dishonest and had subsumed the God who had created the universe to a God that – no matter how unconsciously – we had conformed to our own image. It was a deceit. We saw it in the workers and we had never seen it until now in ourselves. I was convicted. How I had shrunk the God I served. He was so much more and beyond my understanding. He saw the end from the beginning in all this chaos. I was a wretch when He found me. I had taken for granted what He had done in me, and I had no part in what He had done. It was the blood of Christ that had made me, all Him and not me. I felt my spirit had awakened. The truth that for me to live is Christ had been suffocated by social conformity. This of course is not a bad thing in and of itself, but the identity as 'missionary', 'Christian', 'wife and mother', had clouded the essence of who I am. I AM a follower of Christ, I AM dead and I AM hid with Christ in God (Col. 3:3), and all else is secondary.

I could not see how our captors could get a ransom when one of our group had been shot. Overheard conversations about killing us or selling us to Boko Haram or other gangs poured terrible images into our minds. Death seemed preferable than selling us on to Islamic militants. Our thoughts and prayers had to address the issue of possible death. Was to die 'gain'? How do you prepare for death in this situation?

Longing to see our sons was constantly before me and having concerns about their future and where they stood with God. Through the same process of being starkly honest before God, He brought me to a place of acceptance. He loved my sons more than I did. He would be faithful to the prayers we had prayed all their lives. I then thought about Ian as he was instantly translated from this realm to the next. We were certain beyond doubt he was now in the presence of his Saviour and would not wish to return even if he had the choice. It was certain that, as the scripture said, 'What no eye has seen, nor ear heard, nor the heart of man imagined, what God has prepared for those who love him' (1 Cor. 2:9).

This had comforted us over the loss of Ian and focused our minds on what it would be like to die. It then took us back to a forensic soul-searching to see if there were barriers and obstacles between us and God. We needed absolute transparency in all areas of our lives before God. There had to be trust, and to walk by faith and not by sight. We read that stark and terrifying script in Matthew 10:37 where 'whoever loves son or daughter more than me is not worthy of me'. We were convicted, having struggled for years not keeping our sons on the throne of our lives. It's natural to love our children without limit or precondition, but there's a fine line between love and idolatry.

Our God is a jealous God and demands rightly to be first in our life. This line had been fuzzy for years but now it had to be sharp and defined. Any parent would understand this struggle. When we were able, through soul-searching and honest prayer, to reach this point, there came a sublime peace that passed all understanding and an accompanying sense of freedom and liberation. Indeed, at that point to die would be gain. God took us on this painful journey to total liberation. It was a privilege. 'I have been crucified with Christ. It is no longer I who live, but Christ who lives in me. And the life I now live in the flesh I live by faith in the Son of God, who loved me and gave himself for me' (Gal. 2:20). This was the truth we appropriated, our lives were no longer our own. 'For you were bought with a price. So glorify God in your body' (1 Cor. 6:20). Ian had understood this and knew he had been bought with a price, a truth that seasoned so much of his conversation. Our resolve was to be tested at three specific points.

First was when we learnt from the one they called the Pastor that the gang were entirely on their own. All the communities and other militants, who they assumed would help and move us if required, had stood back refusing to help. With the gang in this vulnerable position the conversation turned to getting rid of us. This became a spiritual battle, to empty ourselves in prayer of everything before God, to reach the point where death bore no fear.

The second time was after the meeting with the intermediary, when we realized that he must have known that Ian was not with us. As we were transferred back to the hut, the gang members were surprised to see us back and had eaten what little food we had. They, like us, had assumed we were to be released. The days following rolled on with nothing coming from the meeting, and during this period the gang became agitated and were increasingly antagonistic toward us, resenting the delay and us, now frustrated that payment may not be forthcoming. We began to reason that they had to get rid of us as the net, they feared, was closing in. They shouted at us and now blamed us for the inactivity, even discussing trading us to Boko Haram. They took to cocking the gun and threatening to shoot us. We became sport for them.

The third time we feared death, it turned out, was the day we were to be released. Because of the deteriorated conditions and general stress and fatigue, we each woke with an impending sense of doom that time had run out and they needed to get out. Gunboats were everywhere on the rivers, and to be caught would incur a death sentence. There were other times, but these were specific and we had to prepare ourselves. We could not share this. This was a solitary and isolating ordeal, where each of us had to deal with our fears and thoughts individually before God. There was nothing easy about this. Words were not enough. Assent to known biblical precepts were not enough. This was a laying bare of the soul before God with fears, lack of faith, and the pain we would cause our family. They would never know what happened and would have to live with all the uncertainty and imaginings of what may have gone on.

God in His grace brought us to the place of total surrender at these times. After Ian's death the panic and desire to escape took over and clutching the post as we hid in the waters we had no time to prepare, no understanding really of what was happening. If we were to die then it would be prosaic, sudden and without warning. It was by God's grace we subsequently could approach each new threat with submission and an honest laying bare of our heart. In that process we had but the most fleeting glimpse of eternity, where death held no fear and there were no regrets. It was to offer the culmination of one's faith. It went from a process where I did not want to let go of our boys, and a strong desire to live to an understanding of the reality of the life that lies ahead of us as Christians, that death is not the end.

I was aware of how so much of the world still had a hold on me. It's such a fine balance to walk, being grateful and joyful for what God has blessed us with and making our home here. We wanted to enjoy, but not 'love the world, or the things in the world' (1 John 2:15). We must walk lightly through the world, as sojourners, pilgrims and strangers, looking for a new house, not made with human hands, eternal in the heavens (2 Cor. 5:1).

Even back home it's a struggle to find the balance and continually realign your thinking with eternity. 'Do not lay up for yourselves treasures on earth, where moth and rust destroy and where thieves break in and steal, but lay up for yourselves treasures in heaven, where neither moth nor rust destroys and where thieves do not break in and steal. For where your treasure is, there your heart will be also' (Matt. 6:19-21). This is the eternal and continual struggle for all Christians that we are not laying up for this life, but for eternity. When death inevitably comes to each of us, we then will be ready.

# 13

# PEACE AFTER
# THE STORM

The convoy drove past once familiar villages, Gbalegoror, Opokonou, Oboro and the larger frontier town of Bomadi. This night they looked alien and threatening, a different filter lay across the whole region we had come to love over the past fourteen years.

As the lights faded and we set course for the oil-hub city of Warri, we turned our minds to what the General had asked and what we had agreed. The Mission workers were all local. If we betrayed the General, then would he exert retribution on the team? The General was still free, his gang was large and drawn from many communities and, judging by the empty holdalls in the back of the vehicle, there had been some financial gain. They posed a very real threat to our team.

Equally we could not betray Ian and needed truth to be known and justice to be served. It was a new problem and one we couldn't solve tonight.

In Warri the convoy wove through industrial wastelands and backstreets to a gated compound. The metal gate slid back, and we parked. Still the driver said nothing. We were led into a bungalow, ostentatious and with pieces of oversized furniture that denoted status.

A man in a Homburg hat introduced himself – tall, rather distant and apparently from the State Security Service (SSS) – and announced we would be driving directly to Asaba, the State capital, some three hours away. The intermediary remonstrated. He was tired and suggested quite rightly that we were too. It mattered little, we were going this night. We stood on the shiny tiles in bare feet and stolen clothes, and felt ridiculous against this faux opulence. The men were fractious but the man in the Homburg was adamant.

Once more, this time aboard an ancient Toyota Hilux, we moved out of the compound and headed north, a military escort in front and behind. At the edge of town we stopped. The man in the Homburg got out to answer a phone call. 'Yes ma'am, we're en route now...' His voice faded as he walked away. He sounded deferential.

A voice, soft and gentle, came through the window. It belonged to a silhouette of helmeted policeman.

'Excuse me, I have some water, some bread and groundnuts and Coke Zero. I'm so sorry for all that you have passed through.' He handed the items though the open passenger's window and left for the jeep in front. Shirley commented how gentle his intonation was, so unusual for a policeman who, in this society, has to fight his corner in virtually every aspect of the work.

The trip to Asaba was long. The man in the Homburg hat insisted on having his window wound down, resting his elbow on the open frame. The hot dusty air whistled in the back and our eyes itched and stung. Thankfully, the roads are quiet at night, mainly because criminal gangs operate without impunity, hijacking cars and robbing at gunpoint. Few dared even to step out of the shadows as our armed convoy passed by, and those who did stood as motionless silhouettes against the flames of burning tyres, machetes and staves of wood in hand.

By two in the morning we had arrived in Asaba. We drove past the various governmental districts and compounds for this and that State department, until arriving at a ramshackle, unpainted concrete house. It stood forbidding against the orange sky of Asaba streetlights. The rough-cast concrete wall, even at night, was visibly streaked in blackened mildew. The house looked dilapidated and forlorn behind a vast, rusted iron gate. The horn was sounded and the gate slid back, revealing three large men in full body armour and automatic rifles with night vision sights. Torches were fixed to their helmets, and they stood in silence.

We parked, and Shirley commented that it looked like we had been kidnapped again. What place was this? No explanation, no introduction.

We were told to get out and, as we did so, the door opened and two women came out beaming and welcoming us to their 'house'. They fussed and joked like long lost relatives glad to see us. The man in the Homburg hat had slid into the shadows and we were not to see him again. We climbed the steps into the bright air-conditioned hallway.

Inside, a nervous young man with a stethoscope sat on the couch, a nurse by his side. He stood and greeted us. The gently spoken, armed policeman followed us in. This was obviously a 'safe house' of some kind, and the ladies showed us to our rooms, which had toiletries laid out and traditional African clothes. The whole thing was lovely but surreal.

'Take as long as you like, have a shower and come down to eat when you're ready. I have chicken and jollof rice.' Even at three in the morning this was a tempting offer.

Shirley's hair was a mass of dreadlocks, and it took careful teasing to release them. The clothes were wonderful, colourful and extravagant. When we had washed, we went down for food. The young policeman came up and introduced himself. He was the owner of the soft gentle voice we had heard earlier, and he was a Christian. So too were the ladies, senior members of the Nigerian security force, efficient and personable, whilst at the same time obviously capable and savvy, given they seemed to run the show. Everywhere, mobile phones sat charging and calls came and went. They were patching into phones for intelligence. What seemed homespun on the surface was in fact highly sophisticated, and they knew our workers and all their movements. Encryption and intel on one hand were matched with home-cooked rice and chicken and coffee. It was a clever balancing act, and they seemed consummate at both.

After eating, the young doctor and nurse checked us over, cursorily and almost apologetically.

They seemed surprised we were so well but said they would be back in the morning with some cream for our bites. They were kind and we thanked them.

Though exhausted, sleep was difficult. We checked the door, checked the windows and balcony door time and again. When a lizard fell on the roof we jumped. We hadn't appreciated how hyper-vigilant we still were, and the stillness and quiet was unsettling after the cacophony of the mattress and the nocturnal mayhem of the previous three weeks.

Before we knew it, and as sleep came, so too did the dawn and two further secret service officers, keen to debrief us, each clutching a ring-bound notebook and pencil, looking more like journalistic hacks than special agents.

We sat at the large, polished dining table, Alanna and Shirley in wonderful African dresses, full and flamboyant, I in a shiny male kaftan. At the other end of the table the two men turned over their first pages. Fans swept back and forth as the heat rose.

We carefully retraced the past three weeks before the questions became more closed, more specific, in particular over the person of the General. They asked if I could draw him. The high forehead, outset ears and small beard seemed to confirm to them who they were dealing with.

They asked how Ian had died. We paused, so conscious that this vital detail may jeopardize the Health Care Workers, so vulnerable to retribution. We declined to comment. They gently shook their heads in obvious disappointment and, after another few questions, they closed their notebooks and, thanking us, retired to the other end of the vast living room to talk in hushed tones with their two female superiors.

We sat in silence drained after two hours of detailed questioning and lack of sleep.

'We need to know who killed your friend,' a soft voice whispered into my ear. The senior agent was leaning on the table, her head low, beside mine, but with no eye contact, her chin resting in her hands, her elbows propped on the table. It was a subtle and disarming device. The plea was collusive not confrontational, and the soft voice was calm and measured.

'We need to put a stop to this,' she again purred. 'We need to know...' The voice trailed off.

She then drew silently back and returned to the sofa and her colleagues.

We were in confusion, fearful of endangering the team, yet determined that the truth should be known.

We agreed that the Lord was sovereign and that He was to be trusted to protect the workers. It was not our right to determine what should be known or hidden. We had to place our trust in God.

We called our hosts over and told them how Ian had been shot and the corroborating evidence that confirmed it was the General. They thanked us and immediately began a series of calls to various parties.

Within a few minutes the lady who so disarmingly had completed the debrief offered us phones to call home.

'We need to get you to Abuja. I will see what flights I can secure. Now, you can call your families, please take the phone.'

Shirley had asked several times, but with the interview complete now was the time.

Shirley took her phone. Julian, our eldest son's number was already on the keypad; clearly the Foreign Office had been part of all this.

Shirley walked up and down the hallway, the call connected and the phone rang.

'Hallo,' the voice was Julian's, brusque, expectant, and, with a Nigerian number on his screen, uncertain what this call meant.

'Julian, it's mum.'

'Mum!' The sound of sobbing was immediate, the breaths heaving on the other end. Shirley couldn't speak, the tears immediate and the emotion overwhelming.

'We're okay, we're coming home, very soon.' Words were inadequate and just the sound of each other's voice was more than sufficient.

'We are going to Abuja, then home.' All the hopes and emotions of the past three weeks had been met in that short perfunctory call.

All the flights were booked, and it looked like another eight-hour drive was on the cards. The senior lady looked as disenchanted with the idea as we felt about it and left to make some more calls. She returned a few moments later beaming.

'We've chartered a flight from Asaba to Abuja at two o'clock.' It was now midday. It seemed too good to be true, but true it was.

We left the house together in two jeeps, security guards in one, and drove to Asaba Airport, a vanity project built for the convenience of the State government to ease transport to Abuja and Lagos. Built between two hills, it was a tricky landing and takeoff location. And flights were so infrequent that the car park was empty, and most bays were now growing weeds.

We swept into the entry foyer and passed through security. We were the only passengers in the entire airport, yet the ground staff were the full complement. Televisions, vast and high definition, showed football to every corner of the terminal. Toilet staff and porters leant against desks to watch the game as we moved through to the 'executive lounge', again empty, the vast leather settees waiting for the passengers who sporadically passed through, the seats shiny and without a crease.

I sat and considered the misery of the lives of so many in the Delta creeks. Here was opulence and waste in equal measure. A vast airport costing perhaps more than the Delta communities receive in investment in years, an exercise for convenience, yet without need. Here we were, rescued and receiving such blessings it was beyond comprehension. We were white and foreign. We had currency, currency our brothers and sisters in the Delta would never have been ascribed. Yet twenty-four hours previously we had less currency than our captors, no autonomy, choice or options. It was hard to assimilate.

One thing was clear to us. In each case there was nothing meritorious in and of ourselves. We were merely passive players in each part of this play. We had prayed for weeks that God would have His way with us, and that we would have the grace given to undergo whatever was to be His will for us. It was His will, sovereign or permissible, that Ian was to be taken to the presence of his Saviour; and ours, that we should be being released. But to what end?

Above, a storm was passing overhead and the rain like marbles was cascading on the terminal roof, deafening the sound of the football on the television. A man leant on his mop staring at the slate-grey sky as water poured from the overflowing gutters down the front of the full height windows.

In the Book of Acts, Paul states how God defines the boundaries of our existence. For our brothers and sisters in the work, it seems to be the hardship and trials of the creeks that define their boundaries. Yet for us, a temporary trial, and then a return to another life, our families and safety.

Of course, this too is illusory – we can be robbed of peace, health, security or life at any moment. Ian was testimony of this, but equally, accident, illness and misfortune strike in any context, and the rains fall on the just and unjust in equal measure. But here in the deep sofa of Asaba departure terminal we were privileged beyond all measure. The Word of God states that to whom much is given, then much is expected.

Some months after the ordeal – as I write this with Shirley – there have been times when there is a desire to move on, to leave the events of the kidnap behind, but God spoke clearly that we should never underestimate the importance of testimony and to handle our testimony with great care.

To tell of what God has done is for one purpose only, to bring Him all the glory and honour, and to celebrate His righteousness, and complete 'differentness' to us. We pray, as you have read this account, that you see a God who is so much greater than we can conceive, whose ways are not ours and whose will will not be bent to petitions for our own betterment. Only He knows what is best for us and, truly, His ways are not ours.

The rain was easing and the flight, delayed because of the passing storm, was now ready. We rose and followed the little entourage of the security officers to the departure gate, a glass door to the side of the building. The air was thick and humid, the sky dark and the rain just a light drizzle. We thanked the security team who had been so kind, human and considerate in all they had done for us, and how they looked after us. We hugged them. They both loved the Lord and, unashamedly and with such ease, mixed talking about their faith with the finer points of counter-intelligence. How different it was at home, where to mention the very name of Jesus will bring ire, censorship and protestations of extremism.

Before us on the tarmac sat a white Jetstream executive jet like a white pencil, sharp-nosed and with a side door open. We walked out from the terminal across the tarmac, the rain now falling with purpose, and climbed the three steps. The interior was white leather, mahogany and cramped, just six seats. I sat facing Shirley, Alanna on the other side and two secret service agents at the back of the plane, filming us relentlessly on their mobile phones.

A little cup of chocolates was sunken into the side console, and behind, an air hostess, really too tall to work in such a tight aircraft, sat completing some paperwork.

The door closed and we waved to the ladies pressing themselves against the terminal wall to try and stay dry under the tiny overhang. They waved, turned and made for the shelter of the terminal building.

The engines whined and the plane inched forward before picking up pace. We passed the terminal building and headed toward the end of the runway. The car park sprawled to one side, vast and derelict with maybe two or three cars. At the end we turned, paused and after some exchange on the radio with the control tower, a momentary wait, the release of the brakes and the thrust of the engines engaged. The whine of the engines rose and the speed gathered, the rivulets of water began running horizontally across the tiny windows, the plane shuddering on the uneven tarmac, then silence.

We ascended at a steep angle, bumping, pitching and falling as the pressure within the storm clouds varied. The cloud was low and thick and visibility was quickly lost, the chaotic streets and tin roofs of Asaba fading into grey as lightning flashes surrounded the plane and thunder pounded nearby. The storm buffeted the plane, throwing it around, the timbre of the engines rising and falling, but the plane continuing to climb.

It seemed madness to have taken off in such conditions. The air stewardess checked her nails, unfazed by it all and the pilot came over the tannoy to apologize for the conditions as he began to turn the plane, wheeling upwards through the turbid sky, to avoid another approaching tropical electrical storm that was rolling in.

The irony of crashing in these conditions had probably occurred to each of us but we remained silent.

Then, almost without warning, we emerged from the gloom of the rain clouds into a dazzling skyscape of oranges, reds, even greens, the horizon stretching away and the sun's rays moving around the interior of the tiny plane as we arced once more to regain our original course. The glory of God's creation was laid out before us, the firmament of light and colour as we had never seen before, the blue ascending into the Prussian blue of the atmosphere, and below, the green of the landscape rich and verdant. It was impossibly beautiful and so evidential of a creator who was so vastly beyond our understanding, and yet, just hours earlier, who had, without a shadow of a doubt, informed us that that day He would make a way for us.

I turned from the window and looked at Shirley. She was drinking a coffee from a china cup, at peace and serene.

'Do you remember where you were eighteen hours ago?'

'Yes,' she said, 'on the mattress.'

Shirley re-read the verse that she had held onto all through our captivity: 'I believe that I shall look upon the goodness of the LORD in the land of the living' (Ps. 27:13).

As the plane gently banked north, we gazed at the glory of the colours surrounding us. The two agents were asleep, their heads sunk on their chests. For them it had just been another day.

# 14

# 'WE DO NOT WRESTLE AGAINST FLESH AND BLOOD'

*For we do not wrestle against flesh and blood, but against the rulers,*
*against the authorities, against the cosmic powers over this present*
*darkness, against the spiritual forces of evil in the heavenly places*
*(Eph. 6:12).*

In Ephesians 6, Paul clearly sets out that there is a battle to
be waged by every Christian, with no exemptions, against a
powerful unseen enemy. In verse 12 he tells us we wrestle
against these unseen enemies, but not with flesh and blood.
This wrestling is a fight, a struggle, and is a combat according
to the original Greek word used in verse 12 for 'wrestling'. It
is, in short, Christian warfare.

When Paul directs the fight to be against principalities
and powers, and not men, he is not saying Christians do
not have enemies amongst men, nor is he saying we have no
struggle against our own carnal natures. He is stating that
the main battle is spiritual and against spiritual forces. The
battle is also against the rulers of the darkness of this world,
he tells us.

The darkness indicates ignorance, sin, wretchedness,
paganism and degradation, because we know that God is light

and in Him is no darkness at all (1 John 1:5). This darkness is characterized by selfish, corrupt and base passions. This is the kingdom of Satan. God sent Jesus into the world to dispel this darkness and bring light and redemption to mankind. Every Christian is to be seen as a soldier in this war, and the weapons we are to use are spiritual, described by Paul in Ephesians. When we accept Christ and become a Christian, we are conscripted into His army.

We had been aware of the darkness in the Delta since the first time we visited. Although there are many churches, the darkness is still there and sometimes palpable. Much of the Christianity that is practised is synchronized with pagan, occult and ancient practices. In reality, this is mixing oil and water, and God's presence will not stay where there is mixture. The Bible clearly tells us as Christians that we must come out from among our old practices and be holy as He is holy (2 Cor. 6:17).

When God called us to establish a permanent base at Enekorogha, He began to show us clearly that we were in the enemy's territory. It was a stronghold of ancient practices with roots in an ancient pantheon of animalistic deities and marine spirits, ancestor worship and fetish rituals, where the spiritual profoundly affects the material. These different spirits had created a stronghold in the culture of the Ijaw people and other tribal groups of the Niger Delta region.[1]

Mission in these situations cannot be at the whim of human cleverness and preference, but working with a sensitivity to the leading of God that He would ordain our footsteps such that we would remain sensitive to His leading in all things. Satan is a formidable adversary, and we understood the priority to be led of the Spirit in all matters.

---

1. There is little certainty with regards to the origin of the Ijaw culture and defined people group, but a confluence of research does agree on a migration from the northern Lake Chad region via Benin with some citing a Sudanese and Nile valley origin, again migrating westwards and south, from around A.D. 500. The lack of archaeological and literary evidence means much remains speculative.

This did not mean avoiding fetish and occult places, but that if we were to visit, it would be very clearly of the Lord's leading and with it, therefore, His protection. Many village medical outreaches were held in truly dark and malignant hamlets in distant creeks, but each time there was, through prayer and seeking the Lord, an ability to minister medical help and preach the gospel without recrimination. Some communities had suffered arson and militant incursions, were centres of demonic worship, animal sacrifice and ritual child abuse. We treated the victims of such. Throughout, we had access and God's protection as we waited very intentionally on His leading. It should be remembered that no white foreigner would have ever had entered this region without considerable armed presence, and yet for fourteen years we had unfettered access to the darkest and most remote communities in the creeks and swamps of the Delta. Many times seemingly insurmountable opposition was pushed aside by the hand of God.

On an early trip, having arrived at a community for a medical and gospel outreach, we had to walk some distance from the boat to a makeshift building and rickety public address system. The walk was beside the river, weaving between the bank and thatch houses. Though the distance was short, our senior worker told us to take a longer diversion that threaded its way behind a small thatch shack that lay on the path facing the river. It had tall bamboo poles with thin ribbon-like flags in white and red fluttering in the breeze. The ground before the windowless hut was flat and well-trod. We did as he said. We asked Victory why we couldn't take the straight path but instead this muddy unused track winding behind the structure. He explained it was because of Shirley, that this was the fetish shrine of the community and women could not walk in front in case they were menstruating. As we passed by, we caught a glimpse of a tall, seated and featureless white clay figure in a hat facing across the fast-flowing Niger. The air was heavy with a pungent smell of decaying fruit and alcohol, offerings laid on the threshold. This was one of the first introductions to the ancient deities that had such a hold over the people of this area.

Shirley remonstrated that, not menstruating, there was no need to divert, but Victory cautioned that it would cause a violent eruption, and that people had been killed previously for such violation. It would endanger all the party, so we complied, not wishing to miss the opportunity to preach the gospel.

We set up an area for medical treatment, the community ravaged by appalling childhood mortality and needless loss, where education was non-existent, the school derelict, and superstition and fear pervaded the entire village. The only source of medical help was the local witch doctor and native healer, using bogus methods of cutting and applying kerosene, chilli and acid to wounds and infections.

We set up a white plastic table for the pharmacy, David and Lawrence Oghumu, a local missionary doctor, sat at two smaller tables to see each patient. Shirley and George, a visiting Pastor from Falkirk in Scotland, sat at the opposite end of the room to pray for those unable to be helped medically. Pastor Waive, our local contact, who had been evangelizing the region and who knew the area well, presented the gospel to a vast crowd spilling out of the building, drawn by the promise of health care. While he preached the gospel, two strange things occurred, strange that is to western eyes. The first was a young lady maybe in her late teens being brought to the front in a wheelbarrow. You could smell her before seeing her, the smell sickly and stifling, a stench of decaying flesh. She was skeleton thin, and without doubt it was a wonder she was still alive, her dress stiff with dried bodily fluids and exudate from infection. She had the stigmata of someone with advanced AIDS, oral thrush and concurrent infections. It was a pitiful sight.

The second bizarre sight, following on her heels, were four or five men dressed completely in yellow sou'westers and wellington boots, the hoods over their heads. Outside it was blazing sunshine and sticky and hot, December being the dry season. They filed in and stood silently at the back of the hall, their arms folded. Everyone's attention was on the harrowing figure in the wheelbarrow and, even for the crowd, the smell was overbearing. Pastor Waive, our Nigerian doctor colleague, and I gathered around her, eliciting her history and discussing what could be done for her. In reality there was little that could be done without anti-retro virals, and considerable input from the infectious disease experts at a teaching hospital. There were no veins to find and cannulate, and even intramuscular injections were too painful, her body so emaciated. This was the first of so many patients we have seen over the years who present so late, ravaged by diseases that would have been treatable if seen earlier. But now, after hours or days of worried family members paddling the patient to our clinics, they succumb and die within hours of arrival, their loved ones bereft by the effort to bring them and the rapidity of their demise.

This was to be the case with this young girl, her eyes half closed, murmuring answers to the Pastor's gentle questions, the flies gathering around her eye lids, too weak to brush them away.

We are but human and so often have little to offer in these situations, but a touch to the unclean, a gentle caress, and to tell of the love of a God in the gift of His Son bring a whole new dimension to the care of the dying. The Pastor's gentle rich voice whispered to her of God's love and then gently and with purpose, he laid his hands on her shoulders. He was visibly moved by her condition. This, in itself, was a powerful witness to the crowd who watched on, and a comfort to the dying girl.

You can argue that illness comes from Satan or the direct consequence of living in a fallen world. What cannot be disputed is that the rejection, avoidance and complete lack of compassion are from the realm of darkness. What a stark contrast when we think of Jesus Christ when, in human flesh, He walked the earth, drawn to the untouchables and unlovable.

He elevated the position of women, seen at the time as chattels of their husband or father, and made a line for those on the peripheries of society; and we read of His care and compassion and at times being moved to tears by the condition of the sick and dying and, in Lazarus's case, the dead. These are the two worlds that coexist on this earth, the world of light and of dark. The care and compassion shown by the Pastor, the holding and caressing, displayed more of the gospel of Jesus Christ than any of the words that were being delivered to the crowd. This is part of our engagement in spiritual warfare, to see the people and humanity, though in a dire state, as those for whom Jesus died. We are exhorted to see the person rather than the demonic expressions that may be apparent in their lives. Indeed, our warfare is not with flesh and blood.

Shirley became curious about the men hovering at the back of the hall, dressed for rain, disengaged from the proceedings, and certainly not interested in the presentation of the gospel. Why would they be dressed for a storm, they looked almost comical? The response to Shirley's question was not comical. They were a group of local witch doctors, who were not happy at the provision of medical care. It was an incursion into their own domain. They were the ones to provide any medical care, and with this came control and revenue. It was explained that they had undertaken rituals to call down heavy rain to stop the outreach and hinder our travel. Our boat was open and heavy rains had previously almost sunk it. They knew this. During these tropical rains all activity ceases, the noise on the tin roofs deafening and voices are drowned out. The static in the air will often blow electrical circuits and fry equipment so the outreach and preaching would have to stop. Their attire was a statement of their faith to the forces that they served. This was sobering, to see people who served false gods, walk out and live out the faith they adhered to. We had to ask ourselves, how many Christians would adopt a similar statement of faith in their God to the point that they may look foolish to the people around them? We regrouped ourselves and prayed about the situation, that if we were to continue in this place, then the Lord would be our sufficiency.

With that prayer we were at peace but felt that He had brought us there and therefore would be in control of all, even the weather. So we continued, and indeed rain did arrive, albeit more like an April shower than a monsoon. In the stifling heat the rain was a welcome respite. We felt the urging of God to go out and enjoy the relief of the cooling rain. We stepped out with raised hands and gave thanks for the relief it offered from the oppressive heat, dust and debilitating humidity.

Even some of the workers showed surprise when we did this. They asked us to come in, but we declined, saying, 'What you do not understand is that we love the rain, the heat is too much, and this is a gift from God that we will enjoy.' When they saw our exuberance, they joined us, and at that point we were able to tell them that what the witch doctors hoped would be a curse on us, frightening us, causing us to withdraw, we saw as a blessing and relief. At the sight of us rejoicing with our workers in the rain, the men left, angry and visibly disappointed. God had showed spiritual warfare in action again. As it is written in Genesis 50:20: 'As for you, you meant evil against me, but God meant it for good, to bring it about that many people should be kept alive, as they are today.' We understood that, what the enemy had meant for harm, God had turned around for good, because we had rejected the report of the enemy and put it in His hands. We walk by faith and not by sight.

This was to prove to be one of the first incremental steps in a plan God had ordained for us, to not only recognize the wiles of the enemy but also to deal with them. At the time you don't always see the developing picture but, looking back, this path of training and discipleship becomes clear.

God pierced the darkness in this community at this point, breaking the hold the witch doctors exerted, where we delivered the light of the gospel of Jesus Christ. It was clear that we were dealing with the spiritual realm; we didn't even have to engage the witch doctors themselves. Following this, over three hundred patients were treated, many received prayer, and the gospel went forth. When God calls you, He equips you.

God had led us to pioneer a work in an area of the world we knew nothing about. He called us in our brokenness, and we responded through a grateful heart.

He had put our marriage back together again, and put us back on His path, the path we had wandered from. Every step we took in establishing the Mission was directed by Him. We had no preconceived idea about what missionary work would look like; in fact, we never saw ourselves as missionaries. We had the distinct impression that God had called others to the work before us, and this was confirmed as, over the years, we saw remnants and echoes of failed works where people had started well but then faded and left. There was nothing to recommend or qualify us to the work, simply that we saw what God had done in our life and we simply wanted to please Him with our obedience. We had spent years in self-seeking and disobedience, and now we sought to follow Him and to where He called us. Without precondition and with trust we just said 'yes' to the call.

Our only strength was knowing just how weak we were. In this place your dependence is solely on God. We had to look to Him and His way of doing it, out of our depths as humans from the moment we came to the Delta. God is faithful, in that if He does call you, He will truly equip you. The only manual we had for this missionary work was the Bible; and the only missionary training we received was on the ground; the only mentor, God Himself.

Many times, helping can hurt. Man's ingenuity is powerless against a spiritual enemy. No amount of theories or seven-step programmes can teach you how to serve the living God in an unknown territory. When we accept that any evangelical work is an engagement in the spiritual realm, we must also accept that this work cannot be done without the Holy Spirit. If we engage in this work based solely on the ideas of man and the theories of psychology and social anthropology, we can do more harm than good. What seems right to us from our own cultural perspective can be at complete odds with God's way of reaching a people group. The Bible is sufficient when read and accepted at face value in any culture, in any time. We can learn all we need to know about how to treat people, how to show compassion, how to love the unlovable, how to touch the untouchable. We learn love God's way, for God is love.

God's love is exposing and challenging. He chastens those whom He loves. Saccharin-soaked love of relativist tolerance is a contortion of God's love. He will expose the darkest recesses of our lives. He does this because He loves us. A parent will challenge the behaviour of a cherished child, not to be vindictive but because they want the very best for them. God's love demands truth. As people we will not always apply truth to love, often shielding people from offence by half-truths, bending the truth to avoid rejection, stifling it to maintain the status quo.

In the early hours of one morning, during a regular trip following the wet season, Shirley was woken to pray. This was not an unusual occurrence on camp, often the early hours were the only peaceful times to hear from God. It was unusual, however, to wake with such a heavy heart. God uncovered to her, widespread sexual immorality amongst the workers. It was happening at work, on clinic premises and whilst on duty. Never would this have been disclosed, and certainly not the details. She wrestled with this revelation, but God made it clear this issue must be addressed, immediately.

When David woke, he was startled to see Shirley up and dressed. On waking, he knew something was wrong. She unfolded what God had shown her and he readily affirmed that this was true. The Holy Spirit had witnessed with his spirit too.

It was now early Sunday morning and we were due to take the clinic boat and the rest of the workers to a church a few communities upstream.

David, the Pastor of the local church at Obeinema, was on camp with us. A stiff cup of coffee was required at this point and, as was so often the routine, we sat at the table, waiting on the workers to arrive. Normally devotions were held at 7 a.m. Sunday was the exception, the team arriving in dribs and drabs in time for the boat. The first to arrive was Pastor David. We called him to join us at the table and explained what had been revealed and that the trip to church was to be cancelled. The Pastor laboured the need to get to church, unable to see the gravity of the situation. It was surprising that the first opposition came from a Pastor. It was clear this was to be a spiritual battle. God was clear this had to be confronted; it was serious, and truth could not be compromised to please man, whether a Pastor or his waiting crowds at church.

We called all the workers, and explained they should take their breakfast and come back at 9 a.m. as there was a serious issue to discuss. They seemed shocked and somewhat fearful. It was hard to hold our resolve. Could this be true? Already the enemy was whispering to us that we had heard wrong, and painting scenarios of what devastation this would cause if we were wrong. We withdrew to our room to pray, for leading and strength.

The workforce was gathered in a circle at 9 a.m. sharp, quiet and aware something major was afoot, yet unaware of what was to be addressed. David stood in the centre of the gathering and quietly explained that the Holy Spirit had revealed a situation to Shirley. She then stood and stated that some of the team were having sexual relations with people other than their wife or husband.

As the words finished, a number dropped to their knees weeping, heaving with sobs of conviction, and with cries of, 'It's true!'

Two affirmed, 'Truly God does see everything.'

We were startled by such confirmation of what God had laid on Shirley's heart to share. What followed was a wonderful time of repentance as we gently told them we didn't exclude ourselves from needing to repent, though our issues were different. We were all sinners saved by grace. Now was the time for open confession, without consequence to their jobs. It was a blessed time to get right before God. We affirmed to them this was not a black issue, or white, neither African nor U.K. It was not about accommodating cultural norms. We sat with open Bibles and examined what the scriptures said. Truly God had shown His love by uncovering the truth and all were offered the opportunity of a clean slate, a new start.

Over the next day or so, several came to us individually, seeking prayer to get right with God, a marvellous work of God to witness. There was a new unity within the team. We had engaged another form of spiritual warfare and God had been faithful. We explained that covering truth gives a doorway for the enemy into the work, because he is the father of lies. We moved to the clinic that day and rededicated the building, stating that it was holy unto God. A line had clearly been drawn by the hand of God. Everyone could see this line and from hereon, there would be no excuse.

A few days later we were back in Cambridge feeling satisfied and encouraged by what we had been part of. It had been the usual arduous thirty-six hours door to door, and we were shifting our thinking to what had to be done back home. It was then we received an unexpected phone call. Our senior worker, Victory, delivered a blow, telling us that one of the workers had been exposed very publicly by two women at different times and places in the community for having immoral relationships with them. Both were married, as indeed was our worker. What had remained hidden and concealed despite all our pleadings, God had brought to light. During the time of open prayer and confession he had said nothing, one of the few conspicuous by his silence.

There was turmoil in the community and the name of Jesus Christ had been dragged through the mud, the witness trampled upon. The worker had abused his position whilst wearing the uniform of the Mission. It was a hammer blow. Much discussion and prayer followed. David had returned to work and, the first night returning from work, Shirley was convinced we should return to the community to sort this out. For days we wrestled with the thought and indeed the cost of returning, but within a week we were back on a flight to Port Harcourt and the long drive back to the creeks and the boat trip across to Enekorogha. It was to be a forty-eight-hour stay. We spent this time visiting the families affected, to listen to their grievances and to apologize. We also explained the gravity with which we viewed the situation, that the name of Jesus should be sullied, the testimony of the Mission affected in this way.

The worker was key because he ran the laboratory and we had trained him, taking him to India and Lagos to gain experience in laboratory techniques. This was irrelevant. The line had been crossed, and he had to be dismissed. He knew the line was drawn, and he thought he could get away with things, but God will not be mocked. The testimony and obedience to God's standards is the only thing that mattered, and the very people we were seeking to tell of the gospel needed to see the seriousness of what we held true and of value. To say they were surprised at our arrival would be an understatement. The impact of our presence and interest in the people's welfare of those affected was profound. We put up no argument or excuse and humbly apologized for the effect of his actions, and, with such, God's peace descended upon the community, healing many wounds. This aspect of spiritual warfare aside from prayer involved merely being obedient to the leading of the Holy Spirit. It meant not counting the cost of the inconvenience, the financial cost, the physical exhaustion it caused, and disruption to work commitments at home. This was a very practical application of what it means to 'wage a good warfare' (1 Tim. 1:18). As a postscript to this incident many workers called us to affirm individually that they were convinced that this was God's work, uncovering publicly what should have been uncovered privately, a precept repeated in the Gospels: 'For nothing is hidden that will not be made manifest, nor is anything secret that will not be known and come to light' (Luke 8:17).

Over the years these and many other situations taught us to look to God when human wisdom was inadequate. He had been teaching us that the Christian life is a continual battle. The battle must be fought on His terms and not ours. The cross of Calvary was where the war was won but the skirmishes must still be engaged in, actively, by the Christian.

We found it easier and clearer to actively engage in these skirmishes when we saw ourselves as 'strangers and exiles on the earth' (Heb. 11:13). We are soldiers placed behind enemy lines, vigilant and watchful, given this is not our homeland. We are sojourners. It is only when we forget these truths that we can become complacent and at home in this world. The enemy's tactics are always to get our eyes off the truth of who we are in Christ and to make us feel at home in this world, for Paul tells us that we 'are dead and our life is hidden with Christ in God' (Col. 3:3).

We cannot afford to neglect the reading of God's Word and the continual alignment of our life with His truth. To become overconfident or complacent in these pursuits is to enter a dangerous arena. As Churchill stated in a radio address in 1941: 'Next to cowardice and to treachery, over-confidence, leading to neglect or slothfulness, is the worst of martial crimes.'[2]

We must always live our lives with the continual awareness of the spiritual battle that surrounds us. On the 13th October 2017, the battle was to be brought to us once again. Ostensibly a kidnap for ransom, it became clear it was more. The loss of Ian changed the game. Until this point, our human ingenuity thought we could negotiate with these people. We reasoned they would realize they had taken the wrong people. Surely they knew we had no money. Surely they knew we treated their people. It was almost 100 per cent certain we had treated one of the families of the men who had taken us. For fourteen years our profile has been our security. We were medical missionaries, coming only to serve and expecting nothing in return. We were not oil workers, politicians or anyone else who held sway over vast sums of money. Surely reason and explanation would see our release in a few days.

With Ian's brutal murder, all human reason failed. What really was happening? With our minds in complete disarray,

---

2. Part of the script for a speech broadcast by Prime Minister Winston Churchill on 9 February 1941.

we had come to the end of our selves. The Holy Spirit spoke to us, bypassing our rational minds, ministering directly to our spirits. We were reminded we were in a battle, and, however our physical person felt, we had to engage with this conflict spiritually. At this point past successes in spiritual warfare equipped us in an almost automatic fashion as to how to engage; like a well-trained soldier, whose training is so ingrained and reflexive that in the most adverse circumstances he can engage automatically.

We were not simply dealing with deranged young men. Their profanity against Ian, against us and our Christian faith, indicated this was an encounter with the powers of darkness. There was not time to recover from the shock of the shooting before the new threats on each of us, with a very real chance of both rape and murder following. How do you engage as a Christian in this situation? We must acknowledge that God is still sovereign in this situation, even in the taking of Ian so abruptly. There was a purpose in all that was happening, though it was obscure to us. The choice must be to either trust your whole being to Him or surrender to the fear. We chose the former, again like the well-trained soldier, automatically. It was not an option to capitulate to fear, but we looked unto Him as the author and finisher of our faith, our everything. We turned this around to realize our lives were not in the hands of men but in the hands of God; comfort and scripture flooded us with assurance that they could do nothing without God's permission. We did not rail against God but trusted that He knew best. If we were to ever get out of the situation it would be His hand that would lead us. It was not lost on us that, with Ian dead, a lot of the bargaining power for our release had been lost.

The following day, waking on the new platform, we all lay facing away from the men, avoiding eye contact as we were subject to raucous threats and intimidation. It was as if they had landed a prize fish and were jubilant at their catch. In a sense that was true. Our natural instinct was to stay small and avoid attracting attention or their gaze in any way. For most of that day, still soaked from the flood, we did exactly that, unable to move from the mattress. The Holy Spirit showed us, however, that this was not the way we should be. We were not to be afraid of them. We were not to be intimidated. The more we showed fear, the more they fed off this and the weaker we became. God showed us, 'Little children, you are from God and have overcome them, for he who is in you is greater than he who is in the world' (1 John 4:4).

The prompting was to sit up and not cower, to gather ourselves together, hold hands and pray out loud in the sight of the men. We were to give thanks to God and to put the whole situation into His hands. This we did in full hearing of the men. This was our engagement in the warfare; it didn't entail debating with them but simply speaking to our God. 'Give thanks in all circumstances; for this is the will of God in Christ Jesus for you.' (1 Thess. 5:18) We gave thanks regardless of our emotions. We were prompted to reach for the Bible, the gift that Ian had bestowed on us. Alanna read out loud from the Psalms. This was spiritual warfare. Our weapon was the Word of God: theirs was a Chinese AK-47.

Most days we had the propensity and the desire to let self-pity have full reign. The battle was on two fronts, not only against our captors but also the enemy of our own flesh. We had to fight justifying anger, bitterness and outrage, putting it at the foot of the cross where it was paid for. At times it was an exhausting battle. Every day we had to push through, to pray and read the Bible out loud. This was God's direction, this was the way we would fight this battle. And it worked.

'He must increase, but I must decrease' (John 3:30). We learnt to increasingly empty ourselves and found in it a sublime peace.

# 15

# 'LIKE A THIEF IN THE NIGHT'

*And while they were gazing into heaven as he went, behold, two
men stood by them in white robes, and said, 'Men of Galilee,
why do you stand looking into heaven? This Jesus, who was taken
up from you into heaven, will come in the same way as you saw
him go into heaven.'*
(Acts 1:10-11)

The second coming of Jesus Christ, as Paul explains in
Titus 2:13, is our 'blessed hope'. As Christians we are exhorted
to be aware of the return of Jesus, and to watch therefore, as
stated in Matthew 24:42, for 'you do not know on what day
your Lord is coming'.

Jesus expects His church to be ready for His return, whenever
it may occur. As we are told, no man knows the hour. In Matthew
24:36 we read: 'But concerning that day and hour no one knows,
not even the angels of heaven, nor the Son, but the Father only.'

Therefore, as the people of God, we must live our lives
in a manner pleasing to God, in readiness for the appearing
of our Lord and Saviour Jesus Christ. Our garments should
be without spot or wrinkle. Ephesians 5:27 makes this clear:
'That he might present the church to himself in splendor,

without spot or wrinkle or any such thing, that she might be holy and without blemish.'

This should inform our daily living, as a bride in ancient Jewish culture waits for her betrothed to come and collect her to bring her to the place he has prepared for her. She never knows what day this will be, but is ever watchful with great excitement, for the culmination of her wedding. So, too, must the church look for the bridegroom to arrive.

Many churches do not teach the second coming of the Lord Jesus Christ. Many Christians do not have eternity 'stamped on their eyeballs' as Jonathan Edwards prayed, saying:

> Where will all of our worldly enjoyments be, when we are laid in the silent grave?
>
> Resolved to live as I shall wish I had done, when come to die.
>
> Resolved, to live as I shall wish I had done, ten thousand ages hence.
>
> Lord, stamp eternity on my eyeballs!

'As we look not to the things that are seen but to the things that are unseen. For the things that are seen are transient, but the things that are unseen are eternal' (2 Cor. 4:18).

It's very easy as Christians for us to drift away from this eternal truth. Normal demands of daily living, and increasing bombardment of knowledge, information and the business of life can dull our sensitivities. Whilst we can know these as truths, we can unintentionally become distracted. Solitude and silence are more associated with the past than the present. Often our faith is assailed from every direction, dulling our sensitivity to the Spirit of God. It can take us to a place of complacency, comfort and apathy. In such condition we are no longer soldiers, armed and ready to engage the enemy. We are too comfortable in this world to consider the world to come.

In the early hours of the 13th October 2017, a graphic illustration of a scripture took place, 'For you yourselves are fully aware that the day of the Lord will come like a thief in the night' (1 Thess. 5:2). During the twenty-two days captivity, we often reflected on the manner in which we were taken. We sought understanding from God on why it happened as it did. After fourteen years of peace and safety, truly it felt like sudden destruction had come upon us as verse 3 of the same chapter of 1 Thessalonians states. As we read the scriptures daily, this powerful picture would come back to us. We sought God as to what He would have us learn from, not only the kidnapping, but also the way in which it took place. It was deeply impressed on us that the events of that night had deeper significance than the surface narrative.

We slept behind high walls, metal doors, grilled windows and floodlights. For years we had borrowed shacks and derelict houses but now we had a secure, comfortable mission house, yet it was here that they took us from. We were now working through the scripture given to us on the flight and how it pertained to us personally. In that process we realized that we had become complacent and ceased to be as watchful as we used to be. God was dealing with personal issues in each of us, shining a light on areas of our life and our hearts that needed to be dealt with and chastening us as a father. He inspired us to rejoice in this process, and to count it a privilege.

These separate pieces began to come together as fragments of a fuller picture, a process that continues. We saw our abduction as a microcosm of what the church could face if it is not watching for the return of Jesus Christ. 'What does this mean, Lord?' Shirley asked repeatedly to all that had happened.

This is my church was the answer, not ready, not dressed and stumbling in the darkness, unprepared. Yet we knew the scripture from 1 Thessalonians 5:4: 'But you are not in darkness, brothers, for that day to surprise you like a thief.'

Verse 6 expands it more: 'So then let us not sleep, as others do, but let us keep awake and be sober.'

We seemed to see a picture of the Western church having lost its way in part, with emphasis on prosperity, your best life now, and what God can do for you. It was a frightening picture. A man-centric church was not the church He was coming back for. We believe it was a warning from God and a message pressed upon us to share at any opportunity with the body of Christ. It was time to clean up our act. We should, as 2 Corinthians 6:17 states, 'Therefore go out from their midst, and be separate from them, says the Lord, and touch no unclean thing; then I will welcome you.' And as it is written in 1 Peter 1:16: 'You shall be holy, for I am holy.'

'Thus says the Lord, "Stand by the roads, and look, and ask for the ancient paths, where the good way is; and walk in it, and find rest for your souls".' (Jer. 6:16)

Through our experience it impressed upon us the singular need to rely upon and trust in the infallibility of the Word of God, and in its ways to walk therein. It is vital to take the full council of God and not pick and choose, for Paul himself says in Acts 20:27 that he did not shrink from declaring the full counsel of God.

# 16

# TABLE TALK

This last chapter is simply a collection of our thoughts, conversations and reflections shared, since returning home.

## The General

We were puzzled what this man would do with the ransom money, where he would store it in rickety huts in the swamps, and whether his gang would turn on him. He was rogue for some weeks but ultimately was shot as he tried to escape following arrest, his gang setting up an ambush for the army unit who held him. All but two of the gang were killed. Abe, the young man who enquired so seriously of the gospel, had fled after our release and survived.

The circumstances surrounding the General were muddled and we had no certainty that he hadn't escaped. Reports varied but, by coincidence, David the Pastor had taken his son to the hospital where the General's body had allegedly been taken. I needed closure on this matter and, through certain parties, we accessed a photo of his body in the morgue. It gave no pleasure. I knew where his soul had gone. God had given us a compassion for this man, tired of life in his own words at the ripe age of twenty-seven. It was pathetic, a wicked waste for the havoc and misery he had reeked, and lives taken. Shortly after our release, he had discovered an undercover government agent on the look out for him. He killed and beheaded him, parading and dancing his head through communities. He was lost in every sense. It was chilling and disturbing what man was capable of. (David)

\* \* \*

When we arrived home we spoke often of the men who took us. We had managed to deliver the gospel to the men on the platform, but it had bothered us we had never been able to engage with the General. We were told several times never to address him, and with distance there was a certain compassion for him. When we heard of his arrest, there was initially shock, relief and then pity, knowing he would receive a death sentence and that hell was awaiting him. We felt there was unfinished business and resolved to visit him in jail, reckoning he was a captive audience and would have to listen, the balance of power reversed. It seems ridiculous but it was a strong leading. Learning he had been killed, there were no details of why and by whom. The impact of the news shocked me, and later that day we were having two friends over for lunch and busy cooking. I broke down with pity for him, the opportunity to share the gospel lost. He was no older than my sons and, barring a miracle, he was now in hell, and I wept. When our friend arrived, a floodgate opened and I told her. She was bemused why I would cry over a murderer. I reflected on it, but my heart was breaking for the very same thing that broke God's heart. (Shirley)

\* \* \*

### The After-effects

Offers of help and counselling came from all directions. Kidnap U.K. had contacted us, Terry Waite very kindly offering to talk with us, and many complete strangers called to offer support. It was a surprise to us as much as to others that there was no profound effect on our mental health or spiritual wellbeing.

We reflected then as now, how God had undertaken to heal us even whilst in captivity. There was one bad dream and one time I started at an outside noise after getting back, but we marvelled at God's grace during that period. I attribute my physical well-being and mental well-being to the hand of God through the prayers of many, for which we will be eternally grateful. I also mused how few take prayer seriously when it is such a powerful weapon in the hands of God's people. We still reflect on days in captivity when we knew people were praying for us. If only people realized the power of prayer. (Shirley)

* * *

There was no PTSD, but I found I was reliving every tiny detail of certain days, including Ian, not with anxiety or distress but, in a sense, seeking to understand the meaning behind every nuance of what happened. Kelly, a good friend and a godly man, a retired school teacher in the creeks, called me and soberly congratulated us that we were counted worthy to suffer for Christ's sake. I hadn't really considered it a privilege, but he was right; it threw into relief the whole of life, my own sinfulness and weaknesses and the simple 'otherness' of the God we serve. The experience forged a stronger union with Shirley but beyond that, a more serious acknowledgement of God's grace and mercy and that He had afforded us another life. Each day I am both thankful for all the blessings He gives us, but also the responsibility of redeeming the time and living for His glory. (David)

* * *

My Christian walk can never be the same again, there's a seriousness about God's Word and we don't have the right to take it lightly; we do so at our peril. It shakes you up considering your life being taken, but then why should that be? One of the hardest things to agree with is that of Paul stating, 'for to me to live is Christ, and to die is gain'. When life is good and we have our needs met, can I truly say that?

It's now something I keep at the front of my mind and appropriate on a daily basis. This can only be done when I grasp hold of Jesus Christ the person. There's a pressing need for me to return to my first love, to forget religion, and not be ensnared by the trappings of religion, not to be boxed in by expectations, and not to seek to remain respectable. I have to be prepared to be a fool for Christ, and to please Him and not man. I'm not going to compromise for anyone, nor anything. My goal is to keep my eyes fixed on the author and finisher of my faith. I'm not quite there yet, but truly there's nothing else that matters. (Shirley)

\* \* \*

After we got back, we learnt our team, the health care workers, had not moved from the mission station the entire time, and settled in unity and prayer for our release. At home, churches across various communities and denominations were gathering to pray together. We learnt that for all, their prayer life had become much deeper, and those close to Ian have developed a particularly deeper faith and desire for truth, Ian's death adding a new urgency and seriousness to what they understood it was to be a follower of Christ. Equally our team have become more urgent in the work and, though the gospel has always been preached before clinic opens each day, the patients now know a man gave his life for this message and they listen with new attention and purpose. Amazingly, a new revival began on the back of Ian's murder, with people's ears seemingly unstopped, considering seriously the gospel of salvation and what it means to be alive and human in all so brief a life. Ian's death has brought fruit, and this account is but one example. (David)

\* \* \*

We always told our team one day we may not be able to return, and the plan was always to raise up missionary workers for their own people. It is all of God and we are but cogs in the work. Even after a year the clinic is under armed protection and the region volatile. The work is thriving and the team shares a unity of vision to serve God amidst their own people, and this is how it should be, as we step back; yet truthfully we miss them deeply. We love the team and love the people of the Delta. It is a stressful, difficult place, and much maligned, but God equips those He sends and He equips us with a deep love for the people to know the love of God expressed through His son. We long to see the team again – they are dear brothers and sisters in the Lord – but we speak daily. The future is in the Lord's leading and there is a season for all things, but our commitment is unwavering. (David)

\* \* \*

Following our release, we felt God nudge us to take time out to seek Him, to process the events and indeed write this testimony. The prospect was daunting to leave friends and familiar surroundings and to move to a remote location in Scotland. As often is the case, we can't see what God has in store if we are obedient to follow Him. In this case obedience has brought us to a place of great peace and rest in Him, He's teaching us new things because we have no distractions and peace to hear from Him. It's easy to see how you can get swept up in activities for activities' sake. I think God is calling His people to a closer, more intentional walk with Him. He has much more in store than our small minds can conceive, and He is enough. (Shirley)

\* \* \*

My mother, at the age of ninety-five and still sharp as a pin, had terminal cancer, and inevitably our kidnapping was an added burden for her. The outrage I felt on the mattress both for her distress and that she may die before, and if, we ever got released was a real burden daily. God kept her however, as if her illness had been put on hold until our release. We had batted the gospel back and forth for years, her formidable intellect just unable to accept the simplicity and indeed – and this may have been the major stumbling block – the exclusivity of salvation through Jesus Christ. Yet within two weeks of our release she had given her life to Christ and in her final days she was lucid enough to want to pray for her grandson and his future. God was so gracious to tear down her walls of resistance and show such grace, I wonder if our return was part of her acquiescence to the gospel. One day I will find out ... (David)

* * *

We have learnt to be thankful for absolutely everything, and to see something to thank God for every day, even when trials come. To wake up each day with strength, health and breath in our bodies is a gift to thank God for, and never to take this or anything for granted. Life can cease in a moment. No matter what trials we face, God is good, and His mercy endures forever. We don't know what the future holds, but we do know who holds our future, and with each trial He takes us through, we learn to trust Him more. If all we ever did was to thank Him for the salvation He provided, this is enough to occupy us for the rest of our lives, but He daily adds more blessings, and intentionally, we thank Him for every one. My experience is that there's great strength in maintaining a thankful heart. (Shirley)

* * *

Only after we got back did we find out how the kidnap had involved our sons, my brother and immediate families. We had no idea the activity going on behind the scenes, and it's right and proper to give thanks to all the relevant agencies, authorities which God has put in place, and we should rightfully acknowledge their amazing and most human assistance. Most poignant were reports of how our sons had acted with very great dignity, Julian a final year medic and Aidan in the middle of a Master's degree, both involved in gathering money for a prospective ransom, putting everything they had on the line. My brother Patrick was so assiduous in keeping momentum up with the relevant agencies and holding everyone together.

Through the ordeal our families and wider friendships have been tightened and blessed. The consequence of Ian's murder is incalculable and words in this account will be insufficient to express the loss. (David)

# INFORMATION ON
# NEW FOUNDATIONS

Established in 2003, we are non-denominational Christians who simply believe the Bible and the plan of salvation for man through the atoning sacrifice of Jesus Christ. We seek to live our lives in the light of this truth where faith and action must inevitably meet.

New Foundations works at the community level across many villages in the riverine region of the Niger delta. The region has little infrastructure, is politically volatile and has very little in the way of medical and health services. Oil politics remain a stumbling block to real development, resulting in high childhood mortality and grinding poverty for the majority.

Primary Health Care programs underpin our work emphasising public health education, treatment of the main infectious diseases that cause such high infant mortality, safe birthing practice, trauma care and acute malnutrition. Training is by experiential, on the job apprenticeships, e-learning and bespoke training in line with World Health Organisation guidelines. We have a New Foundations training manual with 120 films transferable to smartphone. Our workers are all indigenous community members. The training course has the State Primary Care Department approval.

Fundamental to the work is evangelism and discipleship. The workers regard themselves as medical missionaries to their own communities.

Besides Primary Care we run social and community programs, a primary school, power generation, farm, and a Microfinance initiative. We also run a small fellowship at the mission station to disciple and encourage new Christians.

Further information about the Mission and ways to support the work can be found at www.newfoundations.org.uk

Also available from Christian Focus
Publications ...

STEVEN J. LAWSON

WHOEVER **DOES** NOT
**CARRY** HIS OWN **CROSS**

# THE
# COST

AND **COME** AFTER ME
CANNOT BE **MY** DISCIPLE

What it takes to follow Jesus

# The Cost
## by Steven Lawson

Nestled in a few verses in Luke's Gospel is a Jesus who would not have been tolerated today: He was not politically correct and He certainly did not try to save people's feelings. Steven Lawson unpacks these few verses, looking at the unashamed honesty, passion, and urgency with which Jesus explains the life-long cost involved in choosing to follow Him. True Christianity is the biggest sacrifice any person ever makes ... but it is in pursuit of the most precious prize ever glimpsed.

ISBN: 978-1-78191-955-2

# THE FIGHT OF YOUR LIFE

## FACING & RESISTING TEMPTATION

### JOHN STEVENS

# The Fight of Your Life

## by John Stevens

The purpose of this book is to help and encourage Christians in their battle against sin, and to ensure that they have right and biblical expectations of the 'normal Christian life'. Many Christians live with a false burden of guilt and failure. They have been taught that the battle against temptation is futile, and that they will never be able to obey and please God. John Stevens examines the glorious promises of freedom from sin in the gospel because of the death and resurrection of Jesus. The 'normal Christian life' is a 'victorious Christian life'; we are daily enjoying far more victory than we might imagine.

ISBN: 978-1-5271-0427-3

REVOLU-
TIONARY
GOD

HOW
KNOWING
HIM
CHANGES
EVERYTHING

JOEL MORRIS

# Revolutionary God

## by Joel Morris

History is full of revolutions, led by people willing to stand up against oppression and lead a movement. People who embody the heart values of the movement. Jesus wasn't a political or military leader, but he did come to bring the greatest revolution this world has seen. For his fellow revolutionaries, Jesus has paid the greatest price. He brings the most incendiary and divisive message you will ever hear or speak about. Will we follow his lead?

ISBN: 978-1-5271-0419-8

# Christian Focus Publications

Our mission statement —

STAYING FAITHFUL

In dependence upon God we seek to impact the world through literature faithful to His infallible Word, the Bible. Our aim is to ensure that the Lord Jesus Christ is presented as the only hope to obtain forgiveness of sin, live a useful life and look forward to heaven with Him.

Our books are published in four imprints:

### CHRISTIAN
## FOCUS

Popular works including biographies, commentaries, basic doctrine and Christian living.

### CHRISTIAN
## HERITAGE

Books representing some of the best material from the rich heritage of the church.

## MENTOR

Books written at a level suitable for Bible College and seminary students, pastors, and other serious readers. The imprint includes commentaries, doctrinal studies, examination of current issues and church history.

## CF4•K

Children's books for quality Bible teaching and for all age groups: Sunday school curriculum, puzzle and activity books; personal and family devotional titles, biographies and inspirational stories — because you are never too young to know Jesus!

Christian Focus Publications Ltd,
Geanies House, Fearn, Ross-shire,
IV20 1TW, Scotland, United Kingdom.
www.christianfocus.com
blog.christianfocus.com